ENCOUNTERING MANAGEMENT

ROBERT J. WECHMAN, Ph. D.
Department of Business and Economics
City University of New York

ISBN 0-87563-306-4

Published by
STIPES PUBLISHING COMPANY
10-12 Chester Street
Champaign, Illinois 61820

To   Stephanie

     Craig

     Evan

     Darren

FOREWORD

It is the intention of this book to provide an introduction to the area of management. It is virtually impossible to cover such a wide area in depth. However, it is imperative to emphasize some of the main aspects of management so that the introductory student can acquire a working overview of the subject. I hope that the students who use this book find it helpful in clarifying the key areas of management.

When one does a study of this sort, a great deal of debt is owed to others. In researching various articles, reports, books and studies, one needs the help of various library professionals. Therefore, I would like to thank the many professionals who assisted me at the libraries of The University of Pennsylvania, Columbia University, Syracuse University, City University of New York and The New York Public Library.

Encouragement is a major part of any undertaking. I have been very fortunate in receiving much encouragement from many students and colleagues throughout the years.

I would like to thank Professors Edward Alexay, Richard Gonzalez, Lambert and Constantine Petrides of the Business Management Department of the Borough of Manhattan Community College of the City University of New York and Professor George Kehr, Chairman of the Economics and Business Department of St. Thomas Aquinas College for their encouragement and helpful suggestions. Of course, any shortcomings are entirely my responsibility.

Robert J. Wechman

TABLE OF CONTENTS

Chapter

*"Nothing astonishes men so
much as common sense
and plain dealing"*

-- Ralph Waldo Emerson

AN OVERVIEW OF MANAGEMENT

What is management?

Management is the process of using people and other resources to achieve goals and objectives by coordinating available resources efficiently.

Managers work with and through other people in getting the tasks accomplished in order to achieve organizational objectives.

Managers can be found in profit organizations such as businesses and non-profit organizations such as government. The concepts of management can be applied to both profit and non-profit organizations.

What are the four management functions?

A. Planning
   This is where the manager:
   1. Determines the goals of the organization.
   2. Determines how future events will affect these goals.
   3. Set up programs and activities necessary to accomplish the goals.
   4. Sets priorities for the use of human and other available resources.
   5. Example - decides how many more coats a company should produce for the next spring season.

B. Organizing
   This is where the manager:
   1. Arranges the human resources of the organization to accomplish its goals.
   2. Arranges the physical resources of the organization to accomplish its goals.
   3. Determines the specialized tasks and functions needed to achieve their objectives.
   4. Example - assigns employees to work in shipping department.

C. Leading or Directing
    This is where the manager:
    1. Leads in the process of guiding people in the activities needed for the production of goods and services.
    2. Motivates people to accomplish objectives.
    3. Coordinates the tasks and responsibilities in order to accomplish the various objectives of the organization.
    4. Example - hiring of employees and ordering of supplies.

D. Controlling
    This is where the manager:
    1. Directs the process by which actual behavior or production is measured against established goals and objectives of the organization.
    2. Compares performance with established standards.
    3. Decides if corrective action is necessary.
    4. Example - a building must be completed by a certain time.

What are the three levels of management?

A. Top Management
    1. Deals with the overall planning of the business.
    2. Deals with long-range policy and strategy.
    3. Work directly with the board of directors.
    4. Made-up of the president and the highest level of executives.

B. Middle Management
    1. Organize and direct long-range plans developed by top management.
    2. In charge of the actual administration and operation of the organization.
    3. Set up procedures for achieving the desires of top management.
    4. Examples of middle managers are heads of departments or heads of divisions.

C. Supervisory Management
    1. Directly in charge of achieving defined tasks done by employees who are not part of management.

4

2. Supervisory managers have direct contact with subordinates.
3. Supervisory managers are in charge of carrying out the plans established by middle management.

Management sets and carries out the policy of the firm.

A. A policy is a statement of principle or a group of principles with certain rules of action that helps the organization to achieve particular objectives.
1. Policy is a guide that helps shape the various actions of the organization.

B. Policy is developed by a combination of forces:
1. Social forces within the society.
2. Economic forces within the society.
3. Political forces within the society.
4. The ethics of the business society.
5. The ethics of society in general.

C. The CHIEF MISSION OF THE BUSINESS MANAGER is to help the business organization produce its goods and/or services as efficiently as possible and to provide the public with fair value at a price that will yield the business organization a competitive profit.

Under the American system, capitalism, which is a system of private ownership and control of the means of production, is viewed as the basis of the American economy.

An honest capitalist is a benefit to society and should be respected as such. He or she should not be degraded, abused, tormented and hounded as if he or she did something evil in making a profit. An honest profit in an honest business is a noble accomplishment and should be respected as such. Profit produces capital, which leads to investment, which leads to productive jobs, which leads to benefits for all of society.

The successful business manager can help benefit America's capitalistic economy by:
1. Producing goods and/or services at a fair value.
2. Encouraging belief in private property and free competition.

3. Encouraging the belief that profit is the proper reward for successfully taking risks in business and providing goods and/or services for the customer at a fair price.
4. Believing in incentives, rewards and penalties in order to encourage progress.
5. Believing in high ethical standards as being most important in good business dealings.
6. Treating labor in a fair manner.
7. Encouraging research and development.
8. Encouraging individual initiative and freedom of inquiry.

D. Is management an art or a science?
1. Science is a body of knowledge that is the product of the use of the scientific method.
2. Art is the skill of doing something that comes from study, observation and experience.
3. Management is the combination of both arts and science. A good manager must have the ability to develop concepts and understand large objectives. A good manager should have skills in psychology, math, business, science, sociology, communication arts and economics.

E. Six key management theories
1. Empirical - theory based on observation and/or experience.
2. Interpersonal - theory based on psychological principles.
3. Group Behavior - deals with how people act in groups.
4. Mathematical Approach - use of mathematical models in coming to management decisions.
5. Contingency Approach - based on how one reacts to various kinds of situations.
6. Systems Approach - uses the systems approach.

F. Scientific Management
1. Uses the scientific approach to solving business problems.
2. Uses principles of analysis to solve problems.
3. Uses planning and the coherent analysis of facts.

4. Action in business is based on fact rather than judgement by "the seat of one's pants."
5. Frederick W. Taylor stated that the fundamentals of scientific management are:
   a. The scientific selection of workers.
   b. The development of management as a real science.
   c. The worker's scientific education and development.
   d. The strong cooperation between management and workers.

G. Key Skills for Managers (from Boardroom Reports, March 9, 1981, p. 6)
   1. Interest in improving methods of accomplishing objectives.
   2. Confidence in one's abilities.
   3. Ability to help others to improve.
   4. Concern with effect managerial actions have on others.
   5. Capacity to lead others.
   6. Ability to inspire others.
   7. Ability to communicate well.
   8. Will usually put business needs ahead of personal needs.
   9. Maintains objectivity in a dispute.
   10. Is aware of one's positive and negative factors.
   11. Can adapt to change.
   12. Able to put in long hours at satisfactory mental efficiency.
   13. Can think logically.
   14. Can use information to create meaningful concepts.

H. "An executive cannot gradually dismiss details. Business is made up of details and I notice that the chief executive who dismisses them is quite likely to dismiss his business.

   Success is the sum of detail. It might perhaps be pleasing to imagine oneself beyond detail and engaged only in great things, but as I have often observed, if one attends only to great things and lets the little things pass, the great things become little; that is, the business shrinks.

7

It is not possible for an executive to hold himself aloof from anything. No business, no matter what its size, can be called safe until it has been forced to learn economy and rigidly to measure values of men and materials."

Harvey S. Firestone
Founder of Firestone
Tire and Rubber
Co.

I. Some key "laws" of management:
1. <u>Peter Principle</u> - a person rises to the level of his/her incompetence.
2. <u>Murphy's Law</u> - anything that can go wrong, will go wrong.
3. <u>Parkinson's Law</u> - work expands to fill the time allowed.
4. <u>M.I.S.S.</u> - make it simple, stupid.
5. <u>Law of Effect</u> - by E. L. Thorndike states that behavior which is rewarded is usually repeated and behavior which is punished is usually eliminated.
6. The <u>Great Jackass Fallacy</u> - is the belief that people are motivated to productivity chiefly by the use of external rewards and punishments.
7. <u>Ergonomics</u> - measure the individual's worth, take his needs into consideration and develop an environment in which he can be creative.

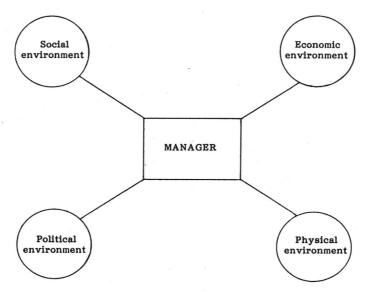

What the Manager Should be Aware of

Decision Making

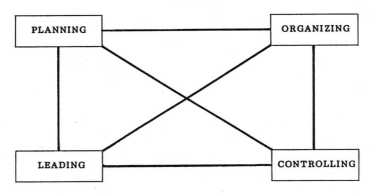

What the Manager Does

QUESTIONS FOR REVIEW AND DISCUSSION

1. Discuss the four major functions of management. Which is the most important?

2. Explain the three levels of management.

3. What is management?

4. Is management an art or a science? Explain.

5. Which of the key management theories do you think is the most useful? Which is the least useful?

6. What is the purpose of managing?

"The danger of the past was
that men became slaves.
The danger of the future is
that men may become robots."

-- Erich Fromm

THE HISTORICAL DEVELOPMENT OF MANAGEMENT

The historical development of management goes back to early times.

I.   Ancient Times
   a.   The Egyptians
      1.   Beginning about 4,500 B.C. the Egyptians showed managerial skill in the building of the pyramids. The managerial skills of planning, organizing and directing are evident in this feat of construction.

   b.   The Sumerians
      1.   e.g. 5,000 B.C. developed written language so they could better manage their assets.
      2.   Had a careful system of keeping records.

   c.   Babylonia
      1.   About 2,500 B.C. the King of Babylonia set up the Code of Hammurabi which set up rules of commerce, contracts and many sorts of business relationships.
      2.   Hammurabi held supervisors responsible for failure of a project.

   d.   The Hebrews
      1.   Moses who led 600,000 Jews out of Egypt during the 13th Century B.C. used the concept of delegation of authority by having his assistants handle minor problems while he handled the larger ones.
      2.   King Solomon developed trade agreements and economic agreements during the tenth century B.C.

   e.   The Chinese
      1.   The Chinese writer Sun Tzu told about the importance of planning for success in military ventures.
      2.   The Chinese also started the use of examinations to find the most qualified people to fill jobs.

   f.   Greeks and Romans
      1.   Viewed with disdain commercial activity but admitted its necessity.

2. The Roman Emperor Diocletion in the 4th Century A.D. reorganized the Roman Empire by setting up two levels of management between himself and the provincial governors.

II. Medieval Times, e.g. 500 A.D. - 1450 A.D.

    a. The Roman Catholic Church was the main institution in medieval society in Europe.

      1. The Church was the predominant influence of land, labor, religion, economics, etc.

      2. The Church was generally opposed to business. It felt that greed was the chief motivator of business and that the pursuit of business objectives turned people away from God.

      3. However, with the growth of cities, there was an increase in trade. With this development, there was a growth of banking, fairs (similar to farmer's markets) and other economic adjustments that the Catholic Church started to change some of its attitudes about the evils of business.

      4. The Church structure laid some of the foundations for modern management. In ascending order

          a. Priest - in charge of a church.

          b. Bishop - in charge of a group of churches.

          c. Arch-Bishop - in charge of a group of bishoprics.

          d. Pope - in charge of the whole church.

      5. The Roman Catholic Church also contrib- to the development of management.

          a. Developed job descriptions for members of the clergy.

          b. Use of staff independence where advisors to a superior weren't chosen by him, nor could they be removed by him.

6. Thomas Aquinas was very instrumental in helping to change the attitude of the Catholic Church towards business. He spoke about the "just price." However, there was still a great deal of opposition by the Church towards general business practices.

b. The Rise of the National State
   1. The rise of the nation-state made things more conducive for business.
      a. New monarchs needed money and businessmen involved in trade needed protection. Therefore, there was an exchange of interests.
      b. In addition the new monarchs needed the support of the business community in their conflicts with the Catholic Church. Here again, there was a mutual exchange of interests between the rising capitalist and the monarchs of the fledging national states.
      c. The nation state encouraged capitalism by issuing currency, developing laws of trade and commerce and giving protection to commercial interests.
      d. The nation-state gave a degree of stability to Europe which was necessary for the growth of commerce.
      e. An excellent book dealing with this period is Tawney, Religion and the Rise of Capitalism.
   2. Machiavelli's The Prince
      a. During the early part of the 16th Century Machiavelli wrote a guide for new rulers. This guide had some managerial principles that are applicable to modern management.

1. The leader should be clear in letting those under him know what their responsibilities are and what he expects from them.
2. Real power is in getting those under you to support you.
3. Clarity in communication is necessary for good, strong leadership.
4. If the rule of the prince is at stake, he is allowed to use whatever means necessary to maintain his power. He can be as tough and ruthless as he sees fit to maintain control.
5. Authority flows from the bottom up.
6. The leader must reward his followers in order to maintain their support.
7. The leader has to set an example for those who follow him.

3. During the era of the rise of the national-states production was dominated by the domestic system, which was characterized by a small group (usually a family) manufacturing some product and selling that product for whatever price it could get.
   a. This was followed by the putting out system.
      1. A middle man provides the materials to the small producer and pays them on a piecework basis. The book Silas Marner by George Eliot is an excellent example of this type of system.

III. Industrial Revolution (e.g. 1700-1900)

    a. The Industrial Revolution was the change from a cottage system (putting our system) of production to the factory system of production. The factory system was the placing of machinery at one location with the workers coming to that place.

        1. The initial aspects of the industrial revolution took place in the textile industry in England and then spread to other areas of western civilization.

        2. Due to abuses in various aspects of the factory system there developed some beliefs in the improvement of management.

            a. Robert Owen (1771-1858) – believed in having concern for human welfare. The conditions of the factory worker should be of conern to management. Owen was an idealist who owned a textile mill in England, migrated to the United States and founded New Harmony, Indiana as a utopian community. He showed the importance of human relations in management. Owen believed that good human relations made workers more productive.

    b. Charles Babbage (1792-1871)

        1. Lived in the early part of the 19th century and is considered to be a pioneer in applying scientific methods to management.

        2. Wanted different parts of the job assigned to workers based on the skill of the individual worker.

        3. Set up guidelines by which managers could compare the value of using machine work or human work. Inquired into the cost of adopting machines versus the use of manpower.

c. Charles Duprin and Andrew Ure (early 19th century)
  1. Early devotees of education for management.
  2. Believed that through education the quality of management would improve and therefore production would increase.

IV. Classical School of Management
  a. Henry Fayol (1841-1925)
    1. Known as the developer of the functional or management process school.
    2. Listed fourteen principles of management
       (1) Division of work
       (2) Authority
       (3) Discipline
       (4) Unity of command
       (5) Unity of direction
       (6) Subordination of the individual to the interests of the whole
       (7) Remuneration
       (8) Centralization
       (9) Definite lines of authority - Scaler chain
       (10) Order
       (11) Equity
       (12) Stability
       (13) Initiative
       (14) Esprit de corps
    3. Fayol believed that the ability to work with "things" was important at lower levels of the organizational hierarchy but the ability to work with "people" was vital at the upper levels of organizational hierarchy.

  b. Max Weber (1864-1920)
    1. Classified various types of authority.
       a) Charismatic-based on the special powers of a leader, e.g., Pres. John F. Kennedy.
       b) Traditional - based on loyalty to the leader.
       c) Rational - legal-based on a system of formal rules.
    2. Believed that organizational design should be a pyramid with a few executive positions at the top and many subordinate positions at the bottom.

3. Each function in the organization calls for specialized competence with appropriate authority.
4. Known for his study of bureaucratic structures.

V. Behavioral School

a. The behavioral school stressed that those who are working in a business organization are the main determinants of the effectiveness of the organization. There is great emphasis on various aspects of motivational theory.

b. Mary Parker Follett (1868-1933)
1. Brought a nonbusiness view to the business world.
2. Believed that real cooperation between capital and labor is the result of the integration of motives and interests that would forge them into one unified group.
3. Believed that the group was more important than the individual.

c. Hugo Munsterberg (1863-1916)
1. Known as the "father of industrial psychology."
2. Was a German psychologist who taught at Harvard University about the turn of the 20th century.
3. He investigated worker's aptitudes and needs.
4. Psychologists can help managers by helping to put people in the right job for them.
5. His chief work was the book Psychology and Industrial Efficiency (1913).

d. Elton Mayo (1880-1949)
1. Known as the "father of human relations."
2. Responsible for the "Hawthorne Studies" of Western Electric in the Chicago suburbs.
3. Concluded that man's social and psychological needs are as important as money in motivating him.
4. Management must take into consideration the human factor in its planning.

e. Abraham Maslow
   1. Known for the hierarchy of human needs:
      Five stages of needs
         a. Physiological - food, clothing,
            shelter.
         b. Safety - security, protection
            against illness, harm, etc.
         c. Love - acceptance, friendship,
            belonging, etc.
         d. Esteem - ego satisfaction and
            gratification, status among
            others.
         e. Self actualization needs - self-
            realization, self-fulfillment,
            to be what a person wants to
            be.
   2. Maslow's theory was published as "A Theory
      of Human Motivation", Psychological Re-
      view (July, 1943), 370-396.

f. Douglas McGregor (1906-1964)
   1. Theory X vs. Theory Y view of management.
         a. Theory X - the average worker dis-
            likes work and will avoid it if he
            can. Therefore, he has to be
            coerced and threatened with fear
            of punishment in order to get
            him to produce so that organiza-
            tional goals can be achieved.

         b. Theory Y - work is natural to man.
            He is self-motivated. He will
            bring self-direction and self-
            control to the job. Man will not
            avoid responsibility and he will
            actively seek it. Man does not
            need coercion and threats of
            punishment in order to success-
            fully produce so that the goals
            of the organization can be
            achieved.
   2. McGregor's theory was set forth in The Hu-
      man Side of Enterprise (1960).

g. William Ouichi
   1. Theory Z is the basis for Japan's phenomenal
      economic achievement
         a. Emphasizes long-range planning.

20

                b.   Decision-making by general agree-
ment between managers and
workers.

                c.   Workers loyalty developed through
guarantee of life-time job.

                d.   Increased productivity is achieved
by involving workers in
solving company problems.

      2.   Key work is Theory Z (1981).

h.   Rensis Likert
      1.   Deemphasized the use of formal authority.
      2.   Encouraged participation in decision making
at lower levels.
      3.   The manager is the key ingredient in moti-
vating the worker.
      4.   He believed that the worker must be made to
feel that he is an important part of the
organization.
      5.   Believed strongly in the human relations
aspect of management.
      6.   Believed that managers are the linking pins
between those they have authority over
and those to whom they must report.
      7.   Chief work is New Patterns of Management
(1961).

i.   Chris Argyris
      1.   Jobs should be designed to fit individuals.
      2.   Matched human and organizational develop-
ment.
      3.   Advocated job enlargement which is increasing
the complexity of a job.
      4.   Believed that the individual should have a
say in what he does and how he performs
his tasks. Workers should be given
information so that they could contribute
to improving performance.
      5.   Encouraged informality on the job.
      6.   His main work is Management and Organiza-
tional Development: The Path from XA
to YB (1971).

j.   Victor Vroom
      1.   "Expectancy Theory" - the motivation of the
worker is dependent upon him believing
that he will receive those rewards which
are important to him if he produces satis-
factorily on the job.

2. His chief book is <u>Work and Motivation</u> (1964).

k. Theory "F" - According to Michael L. Jablow (a U.S. citizen who founded an electronics Marketing firm in Japan) negative factors now play a greater role in Japanese corporations than the type of humanistic principles popularized by such pro-Japanese management supporters such as William G. Ouchi. According to Jablow it is <u>FEAR</u> that moves the Japanese mangers. There is no room for failure. Jablow points out that the choice for an executive who fails is being shipped to a minor post or early retirement. He stresses that fear is the prime mover in Japanese management. Part of this is due to the Japanese culture. The Japanese manager views the firm not only as the vehicle for maintaining a particular standard of living but as the final determinant of his self-esteem. (Kotkin, Joel and Kishimoto, Yoriki, "Theory F" <u>Inc.</u>, April, 1986, 52-60).

l. Frederick Herzberg
   1. Two-Factor Theory
      a. Maintenance factors - working conditions, this will not motivate the worker, but the absence of good working conditions will make him unhappy.
      b. Motivational factors - These are higher level needs, e.g., possibility of advancement, responsibility, sense of achievement, etc.
   2. Herzberg's main work was written with Mausner and Snyderman, <u>The Motivation to Work</u> (1959).

m. Chester I. Barnard
   1. President of New Jersey Bell Telephone Company.
   2. Emphasized the importance of the individual worker.
   3. Understood the importance of using incentives to motivate the worker.
   4. Emphasized the human relations aspect of management.
   5. Believed the organization had to have cooperation in which workers accepted authority by choice rather than by force.

6. Barnard's chief works are The Functions of the Executive (1938) and Organization and Management (1948).

n. Peter Drucker
1. Combined Social Science into management theory.
2. Developed MBO (Management by Objectives).
3. Believed that effective management can be learned.
4. "The main responsibility of managers is to manage productivity of capital." (The Wall Street Journal, July 24, 1975, p. 12).
5. Sees no conflict between profit and social responsibility.
6. Key work is The Practice of Management (1954).
7. Is America's leading authority on management.

o. Joan Woodward (1917-1971)
1. Stated that successful industrial organizations with different types of production technology need different kinds of organizational structure to fit that specific technology.
2. Believed that there are optimum spans of control and this is affected by the type of technology used in production.
3. Key work is Industrial Organization: Theory and Practice (1965).

VI. Scientific Management School

a. The Scientific Management School deals with the application of scientific methods to business. These people see management as a system of mathematical models and processes and rely strongly on the application of scientific analysis to the problems of management. The scientific school presently believes that management is a process of interrelated functions. They believe that management principles are extremely important. They accept the position that there is a universality of management whereas all managers do the same basic functions. Those who favor the Scientific Management School are usually versed in quantitative methods, computer technology and systems analysis.

23

b. Frederick W. Taylor (1856-1915)
   1. Known as the father of scientific management.
   2. Founded the "exception principle" - manager should schedule his workload so that subordinates handle the routine assignments while he gives his time to exceptional problems and situations.
   3. In his book Principles of Scientific Management (1911), Taylor said that managing is "knowing exactly what you want men to do, and then seeing that they do it in the best and cheapest way."
   4. Labor and management should not argue about how profits would be divided but should concentrate on maximizing profits.
   5. Taylor concentrated on the fiscal aspects of business but overlooked human nature.
   6. Taylor believed "that the best management is a true science, resting upon clearly defined laws, rules, and principles, as a foundation."
   7. Taylor favored scientifically selecting and then training the workman instead of letting him train himself.
   8. Believed that responsibility and work should be divided equally among management and workers.

c. Frank (1868-1924) and Lillian (1878-1972) Gilbreth
   1. Looked for "the one best way" to do a specific task through the method of motion study.
   2. Established two major concepts:
      a) existence of basic tasks common to all work operations.
      b) the importance of establishing principles of efficient motion.
   3. Basic unit of motion is called a therblig, which is Gilbreth spelled backwards with the h and t reversed. The Gilbreth's devised 17 basic hand motions.
   4. Lillian Gilbreth was one of the earliest founders of what is now known as personnel management. She believed in the scientific selection, training and placement of human resources.
   5. The Gilbreths were obsessed with time and motion studies and at times they overdid it.

6. Developed the merit-rating system.

d. Henry Gantt (1861-1919)
    1. Developed an incentive and bonus plan to en-
       courage production workers into greater
       productivity.
    2. Developed the Gantt chart.
    3. Tried to combine the human and work element.
    4. Gantt wanted to guarantee all workers a
       daily wage because he believed that job
       security was a strong incentive.

VII. Management Science School

a. Sometimes known as the operations research (OR)
school.

b. This is the application of scientific methodology in
obtaining solutions to problems which developed
in the operation of a system that can be repre-
sented by a mathematical model, and finding the
solution to these problems by using mathematical
equations which represent the system.

c. This school had its start during World War II when
scientists were organized into research groups to
solve various operational problems which the military faced. One of these problems was in determining the correct number of ships needed to
protect a convoy as it was crossing the Atlantic
Ocean and the size that the convoy should be in
order to receive the best protection.

d. The Scientific method included:
    1. observe the system
    2. build a model
    3. observe the model to see how the system
       would react
    4. test the model.

e. The success of the operations research approach was
so, that by the mid-1950s management science
techniques were being applied to such managerial
problems as product packaging, location of plants
and the scheduling of production.

f. The Systems thinking approach to management:
    1. Founded by Ludwig Von Bertalanffy.

2. The key idea of the general systems theory is that a complete understanding of the whole operation of an entity requires that it be viewed as a complete system.
3. A system is an organized group of inter-dependent parts, components or subsystems joined together and functioning as a whole to achieve some objective.
4. Systems can be determined to be open or closed systems.
    a. Open system
        1. is influenced and does interchange with the environment, e.g., a plant.
        2. is characteristics of to-day's firms with their emphasis on inter-change with the rest of society.
    b. Closed system
        1. is not influenced and does not interchange with the environment, e.g., watch.
        2. is not characteristic of most of today's firms.

g. System of components are made up of:
    1. Inputs which are human and physical re-sources that are necessary to operate the system, e.g., people, raw materials, information.
    2. Transformations which are the various steps involved in changing the inputs into out-puts, e.g., the steps in the manufactur-ing of changing a piece of fabric into a shirt.
    3. Outputs which are the final product of the system, e.g., the shirt is the final prod-uct of the manufacturing system in the textile industry.

h. One basic benefit that management believes sys-tem theory gives, is synergy - that the sum of the product is greater than the sum of its individual parts.

i. Key characteristics of open systems are:
    1. Negative entropy-systems maintain their
        strength and fight the tendency to disin-
        tegrate by taking resources that they
        need from the environment, e.g., an
        automobile as it runs down over the years
        takes from its environment to maintain it-
        self (new brakes, new gas line, new
        valves, new tires, etc.).
    2. Feedback - is information used by the system
        to keep track of its performance, e.g.,
        when a manager asks subordinates to
        evaluate a proposal and receives either
        written or spoken reports, or both.
    3. Differentiation - this is the trend toward
        specialization. e.g. law firms in a great
        many instances specialize in just one type
        of law such as matrimonial law, real
        estate law, labor law, tax law, criminal
        law, etc.
    4. Equifinality - is the view that firms can
        achieve their objectives by using various
        courses of action. This requires firms to
        have a certain degree of flexibility.

j. The systems approach helps the manager to focus on
    how all segments of the organization are inter-
    related. Within the systems approach, the man-
    agement system is generally open and interrelates
    with its environment. Among the environmental
    influences which the management system con-
    fronts is competition from other firms. Any or
    all of these influences can alter the future of
    a particular management system using "Systems
    Methodology."

QUESTIONS FOR REVIEW AND DISCUSSION

1. How did the principle of management develop in (a) Ancient Times, (b) Medieval Times?

2. How are Machiavelli's ideas applicable to modern management?

3. How did the Industrial Revolution influence the rise of modern management?

4. Describe the main principles of the Classical School of Management.

5. Why is the Behavioral School of Management most popular today?

6. Can the Japanese method of employer-employee relations be successful in the United States? Why?

7. Which is the most important factor in Maslow's "Hierarchy of Human Needs?" Explain.

8. Compare Theory "X" and Theory "Y". Which one do you favor?

9. Why is Frederick W. Taylor known as "the father of scientific management?"

10. How has the Management Science School contributed to modern management?

11. Which theory of management do you think is the best? Why?

*"The most powerful factors in
the world are clear ideas in
the minds of energetic men
of good will."*

-- *J. Arthur Thomson*

PLANNING OBJECTIVES IN MANAGEMENT

A. What are objectives?
    1. Organizational goals.
    2. The end or purpose toward which managers direct their efforts.
    3. Defines aims of what the business should accomplish.

B. Objectives of a business organization
    1. Survival - businesses work towards staying in business through good or bad economic times.
    2. Produce and/or distribute a productive service - most firms believe that they are producing or distributing a product which is necessary to an industrial consumer market. Therefore, they must see to it that their product and/or service is produced or distributed as quickly and efficiently as possible.
    3. Expansion - most business organizations try to expand, especially in a flourishing economy. They can expand through diversification, producing a better product, successful methods of promoting the product or service, prudent investment of capital, good public relations, community service, providing efficient service for their customers (e.g. IBM Corp.).
    4. Profit - the objective of every company in the private sector of the economy is to show a profit. Profit is a return of money greater than the cost of doing business. There is nothing wrong in trying to make a profit. That is the object of business. As long as the business dealings are fair and ethical, there isn't any evil in striving for, or making a profit.

C. Benefits of Objectives to a business organization
    1. Objectives give direction - they set up a goal towards which management can direct their efforts.
    2. Objectives provide standards - people need something to strive for. Objectives provide a level for prople to try to attain. They provide a standard by which the actual performance can be measured against.
    3. Objectives provide motivation - managers and employees are encouraged to put forth their best efforts in order to achieve various objectives.

D. Functional Objectives
      The successful achievement of particular functional ob-
jectives are the prime method by which the overall objectives of the organization are achieved
    1. Buying Objectives
          a. Knowledge of the sources of raw materials,
              supplies and other materials necessary
              for the successful completion of the
              product and/or service.
          b. Getting the best material at the best price.
          c. Trying to make sure that all material is
              delivered on time.
    2. Selling Objectives
          a. To sell as much of the product and/or ser-
              vice as possible.
          b. To obtain an ever-increasing share of the
              market.
          c. To find and develop new markets.
          d. To increase revenues.
          e. To improve customer relations.
    3. Operating Objectives
          a. To produce the product and/or service with
              greater efficiency.
          b. To increase and improve the quality of the
              product and/or service.
    4. Facilitating Objectives
          a. To maintain the factors of production in
              good working order.
          b. To keep the physical plant in as good work-
              ing condition as possible.
          c. To keep the human resources element in as
              positive a view toward achieving as
              high a quality as possible.
          d. To help other functional areas achieve their
              objectives.
    5. Managing Objectives
          a. To have good management.
          b. Reduce the cost of administration.
          c. Develop management training programs.
          d. Improve morale in the workplace.
          e. Coordinate all aspects of the business.

E. Classification of Objectives
    1. Short-term objectives refers to a period of time of
        one year or less.
    2. Long-term objectives refers to a period of time
        more than one year.

3. External objectives
    a. Service objectives such as service to your customers.
    b. Improve relations with the public as a whole.
4. Internal objectives
    a. Satisfy the needs of various groups within the company.
    b. Improve the quality of the product and/or service.
    c. Improve the marketability of the product and/or service.
5. Social objectives
    a. Provide jobs for the community in which the organization is located.
    b. Take part in charitable projects of the community.
    c. In general improve the quality of life of the community in which the organization is located.

F. Characteristics of sound objectives
    1. Should be understood
        a. Everyone, whether worker or manager should clearly understand what the objectives are.
    2. Should be specific
        a. Objectives should <u>not</u> be vague, unclear or abstract.
        b. Managers and workers should be well aware exactly what the objectives are.
        c. Objectives should be concrete.
    3. Should be time specific
        a. Managers and workers should be aware by what time they should achieve specific objectives.
    4. Should be desirable
        a. Objectives should be worthwhile for managers.
        b. Objectives should be fair and beneficial to all involved.
    5. Should be flexible
        a. Objectives set up at a particular time may not be feasible as times and conditions change. Therefore, objectives may have to be revised over a period of time.

6. Should be challenging but attainable
    a. Objectives should be realistic or else they lose their meaning.
    b. Objectives should provide people with a feeling of accomplishment if they put forth their best effort.
    c. Attainable objectives have proven to be a successful method of motivating people.
7. Objectives should be developed and supervised by those who are responsible for their achievement.
    a. Those in control of their own destiny tend to do a better job.

G. Management by Objectives (MBO)
1. MBO was popularized by Peter Drucker in the 1930's.
2. MBO is sometimes called "Management by Results."
3. Under MBO, attention is directed on what should be accomplished rather than by the methodology or how something will be accomplished.
4. The steps in Management by Objectives
    a. Individual develops description of his or her objectives.
    b. Discussion between the individual and his or her superior in which short-term objectives (usually three months) are established.
    c. After short-term period, subordinate and superior get together to review objectives and make revisions in the objectives if they both agree it is necessary.
    d. At various points under MBO the subordinate and the superior meet regularly to go over the objectives and continue to make changes as necessary.
    e. At established periods, checks are made to establish if there is successful progress towards achieving the objectives that were set.
    f. At the end of the period, the subordinate and superior meet to evaluate the efforts of the subordinate. Reasons for goals being achieved or not being achieved are discussed.
    g. New goals are then set for the next period.
5. Advantages of MBO
    a. Agreement between superior and subordinate on the objectives to be accomplished.

b. Subordinate is encouraged to be responsible for his or her own decisions.
c. Subordinate knows what is expected of them.
d. Subordinate knows the limits of what they can or can't do.
e. Morale may be improved because of the subordinate having a say in what is to be accomplished.
f. Performance is evaluated by what is accomplished instead of how one follows orders.
g. The subordinate gets some freedom to use their own ideas in accomplishing their objectives.

6. Disadvantages of MBO
a. Many managers are not committed to MBO.
b. Increases pressure on the individual without giving him many choices of objectives.
c. MBO emphasizes the quantitative rather than the qualitative in judging the achievement of objectives.
d. Top management usually does not support MBO and if they do they support it in a lukewarm manner.
e. Many MBO programs just go through the motions without any real results.
f. Too much emphasis on paperwork in order to justify MBO.
g. The subordinate receives little help in accomplishing the objectives.
h. Qualitative work is not emphasized.
i. Certain subordinates are not able to work under an MBO system and therefore should not be subjected to it.
j. Many managers do not know how to implement a successful MBO program.

H. Financial Planning (See J. J. Hampton, Financial Decision Making)
1. The process of financial planning is usually called budgeting. It makes use of future financial statements, balance sheets, income statements, fund flow statements and other types of formal statements.
2. Managers also use specific analytical tools that help in planning and budgeting which can increase the accuracy of forecasts of sales and costs and therefore increase the reliability and validity of financial statements.

3. <u>Break-even analysis</u> is used to determine the level of activity at which an orgranization will neither lose money nor make a profit. At this level, the organization is operating at a zero-profit level or break-even point. Break-even analysis uses revenues, fixed costs, and variable costs.

$$BP = \frac{Fixed\ Costs}{(Price - Variable\ Costs\ Per\ Unit)}$$

4. <u>Marginal cost</u> is the cost of producing one additional unit of an item.

5. <u>Marginal analysis</u> is used to determine if it pays to increase production.

6. <u>Profit-volume analysis</u> makes use of the concept of marginal analysis. This is done because profit-volume analysis defines costs and profits using fixed and variable costs. By holding the selling price and variable costs at a constant, financial managers may forecast profits at different levels of sales. Therefore, a company might be able to forecast the net income or net loss after taxes that will probably take place at different sales levels.

    a. In many instances, a company will consider the possibility of charging a few different prices for a new product about to enter the marketplace. An established product will usually be evaluated with respect to the correctness of its selling price. Different prices will usually result in varying levels of unit sales. Lower prices will usually bring more unit sales. The additional sales may or may not result in added profits. The manager has to determine if a reduced selling price if beneficial or not in terms of profit. Therefore, marginal analysis, is used to determine how differing prices affect the net income or net loss after taxes.

    b. In a large number of instances, a firm will have a degree of control over the relationship between fixed and variable costs. If the firm is able to invest in modern equipment, it will increase its fixed costs but might lower its variable costs. If the firm has enough production so that the reduced variable costs

36

provide greater savings than the costs that have increased, the firm will have higher profits by buying the modern equipment. Marginal analysis can predict if this will occur.

I . In financial planning, the company must consider the results of various courses of action on the value of its stock. The courses of action can cause an increase or decrease in the market price of the common shares of stock. Therefore, analysing future earnings per share (EPS) is an important aspect for management to consider.

1. In profit-planning two measures of corporate profits are very significant. A return on investment (ROI), which is a key indicator of profits and success of the managers. This is then compared to the ROI of various competing companies.

a. Earnings per Share (EPS) is a market indicator of profits and is the most significant profit determinant for stockholders. If the earnings increase on a per share basis, the company is viewed as being on the rise while a decline in earnings is looked upon as being a strong indication of problems. Therefore, the company should be aware of how different modes of activity will influence the future earnings per share of the company.

1. When a company debates new investment alternatives, the revenues and expenses associated with the investments will change the projected earnings. Therefore, in determining the result of each project, the company should project EPS without new projects

and then project
each different pro-
posal's effect on
earnings per share.
Comparing future
courses of action at
the margin means
that each proposed
investment is judged
separately to see
how it will affect
the company's sales
and profits.
2. To use the future EPS
approach to profit
planning, the man-
ager should begin
with a forecast of
sales during the
next specific period
without any new
investments. Mar-
ginal analysis is
then used in de-
termining the profit
or lack of profit.

J. Investment in new major projects
1. For a company to invest in new major projects it
must have the capital available. There are four
major choices of financing.
a. Internal funds - if a company has an
adequate cash flow, it may retain a
larger sum of funds from operations
that could be used to finance new
investments.
b. Debt financing - if a firm borrows to
raise money to finance a project, it
will incur interest payments and
these paymetns will decrease the
earnings per share.
c. Preferred stock financing - if this
method is adopted to raise funds,
the dividends which are payable to
the preferred stockholders will decrease the earnings per share.
d. Common stock financing - does not in-
volve any additional charges for

the new project. However, if the new project is not as profitable as the company's present projects, the earnings per share will decrease.

    2. One can see that a company will usually prefer the projects and financing method that offers the greatest future value to the company.

K. Planning the Budget
1. Budgets are plans in terms of number of dollars, hours, units, etc.
2. Budgets are developed in order to achieve company objectives.
3. Budgets are also helpful for controlling operations.
4. A sample budget plan for a manufacturing organization is as follows:
    a. General economic forecast
    b. General industry forecast
    c. General company forecast
    d. Development of budgets
        1. Production budget
        2. Sales budget
        3. Administrative budget
        4. Cash budget.
5. Preparing of the master budget.

L. An effective business plan should have:
1. Clearly stated objectives.
2. Measures of a satisfactory accomplishment of objectives in terms of quality, quantity, time and cost.
3. Definitive statement of policies to guide the people.
4. Indications of which organizational unit will be responsible for fulfilling the objective.
5. Time allotments for each phase of the work.
6. Specifics of the number and nature of manpower needed.
7. Projections for expenses such as labor, machines, materials and methods.
8. Designations of which managers will be held accountable for accomplishing the objective.

M. Characteristics of a good business plan:
1. Objective
2. Clear
3. Concise
4. Simple (MISS - "Make it Simple Stupid")
5. Flexible

6. Stable
7. Integrated
8. Complete
9. Controllable

QUESTIONS FOR REVIEW AND DISCUSSION

1. Why is planning necessary?

2. Why are objectives important?

3. How do objectives benefit a business organization?

4. Explain the characteristics of sound objectives.

5. Explain MBO.
   a) Is MBO beneficial? How?
   b) How is MBO harmful?

6. Explain the role of profit in organizational objectives.

7. Discuss profit-volume analysis.

8. How does scientific planning differ from other kinds of planning?

9. Explain the characteristics of a sound business plan?

10. It has been said that "company planning should include budgeting but budgeting does not constitute complete planning?" Explain.

"I hold that man is in the right who is most clearly in league with the future."

-- Henrik Ibsen

THE PROCESS OF PLANNING

A. What is planning?
  1. Planning is the process of formulating objectives and determining courses of action in order to successfully achieve the objectives.
  2. Steps in the planning process
     a. Determine what has to be accomplished.
     b. Collect and organize the necessary information.
     c. Determine what kind of problems you may face.
     d. Determine what kind of actions you may take if you cannot solve various problems.
     e. Determine the type of plan you will follow in order to accomplish your objectives.
     f. Determine the methods of controlling the plan.
  3. Steps in strategic planning
     a. Strategic planning is the process of determining a business organization's main objectives and the policies that will be implemented in achieving these objecttives.
        1) Determine what are the objectives of the organization.
        2) Determine the values and philosophy of top management.
           a) There isn't any point in setting long or short range goals if it is not coherent with the social and business philosophy of top management because without top management's approval the goals cannot be achieved.
        3) Develop long-range objectives.
        4) Develop methodology to accomplish the long-range objectives.
        5) Develop short-range objectives.

6) Develop methodology to accomplish the short-range objectives.
7) Develop methods of implementing change in the various plans.
    a) Careful analysis of both the internal and external environment is necessary. Special concentration should be addressed to developments in the economic, financial and marketing area.

4. Plans can be divided into three parts:
   a. Time - determines how long the plan would be in effect.
   b. Use - determining the activities that are necessary for the plan to be carried out.
   c. Breadth - determining how much the plan should include.

B. Planning should be flexible
   1. Managers should be able to make adjustments when necessary so that the following questions are answered continually.
      a) Where are we now?
      b) Where are we going?
      c) What problems are we facing?
      d) Can we overcome these problems?
      e) Are we moving in the right direction?
      f) Will we get to where we want to be at the right time?

C. Does planning help?
   1. In 1970 Thune and House analyzed planning in six industries and thirty-six different companies. The researchers attempted to evaluate how effective planning was. They compared companies with formal planning programs with companies that didn't have any. Thune and House found that firms with formal planning programs were more successful than those with informal planning and those firms with formal planning programs, after a formal planning system was

initiated, had a sales increase by 38% and an earnings per share rise of 64%. (See Thune, Stanley and House, Robert, "Where Long-Range Planning Pays Off," <u>Business Horizons</u>, Vol. 13 (1970), 81-87.

2. Random behavior is different from planned behavior. With random behavior one finds that unplanned business activities will be random and without direction towards objectives.

3. Planning uses historical perspectives in coming to decisions. However, patterns of behavior do not usually repeat itself exactly. If they did, planning would be simple. However, there are a variety of variables that determine people's actions. Therefore, planning has to take into consideration various courses of action if there is a deviation from what is expected. A good plan takes this into consideration and provides various alternatives.

4. Planning obviously is a major function of management because, since the future is uncertain, good planning can reduce uncertainty and chances for error. The better the plans the more variables that the firm can control. The poorer the plans the less variables that can be controlled. Nobody can foresee and plan for every conceivable event. However, the firm which has the better plans achieves an edge over those firms who do not plan or who do not plan well.

5. Planning entails setting the objectives of the organization and determining a methodological approach to accomplish the stated objectives. Good planning is necessary in order to avoid the harmful effects of random behavior. By careful planning an organization can be more in control of its destiny than being controlled by destiny.

D. Advantages and disadvantages of planning

Advantages	Disadvantages
1. Focuses attention on objectives.	1. Information may be incorrect.
2. Provides a basis for people in the firm to work as a team.	2. Difficult to predict changes in the future.

3. The firm is forced to adapt to its environment.
4. Helps to anticipate problems.
5. Provides direction in a firm's activities.
6. Helps to make the controlling function easier.
7. Provides alternatives to possible deviations in the plan.

3. Objectives may not have good coordination among various departments.
4. People may get tied to plans too much and this might reduce their ability and desire to maneuver when necessary.

E. Effects on planning
   1. The type of product or service - e.g. different planning if one is selling women's dresses or cereals.
   2. The quality of management
      a. Are they capable?
      b. Do they believe in planning?
      c. Can they motivate their subordinates to achieve success in carrying out their plans?
   3. Size of the firm
      a. The size affects the degree of planning the various managers have on different levels.

F. Key Indicators - In order to plan correctly, managers should be aware of the Key Indicators in our economy. The following is based on "How Those Key Indicators Really Work," U. S. News & World Report, February 7, 1983, p. 58.
   1. Average workweek of production workers in manufacturing.
      a. Employers increase the number of hours worked in a week before hiring more employees.
   2. Initial claims for unemployment insurance.
      a. The number of people who sign up for jobless benefits reflects changes in present and anticipated economic activity. The fewer who sign up, the better.

3. Vendor performance.
    a. This is the precentage of firms reporting slower deliveries. As the economy grows, companies have more trouble filling orders.
4. Change in total liquid assets.
    a. This component shows changes in the amount of buying power readily available. In time, this purchasing ability will be used to buy or invest in goods and assets.
5. Percent change in prices of sensitive crude materials.
    a. Rises in prices for such raw materials as iron and steel scrap or cattle hides usually mean factory demands are going up.
    b. Manufacturers plan to step up output.
6. Contracts and orders for plant and equipment.
    a. After orders are received, manufacturing and construction begin to grow.
7. Net business formation.
    a. When prospects for profits rise, entrepreneurs create new firms.
8. Stock prices.
    a. A rise in Standard & Poor's Corporation index of 500 common stocks indicates higher actual and expected profits and lower interest rates.
9. Money supply.
    a. A rising money supply suggests more funds are available to finance economic activity.
10. New orders for manufacturers of consumer goods and materials.
    a. When such orders are received, workers are hired, materials and supplies are purchased and output grows.
11. Residential building permits for private housing.
    a. Usually several months pass between the time a permit is issued and the start of construction. Increased building permits indicate an upturn in the economy.

12. Change in inventories.
    a. When companies expect greater sales, they build up stocks on hand.

G. Managers need to keep up with the latest figures of such items as national income, employment, and production, among other statistics. For this information to be current, the manager should consult:

The Economic Report of the President. Washington: U. S. Government Printing Office, annually.

The Survey of Current Business. Washington: U. S. Department of Commerce, monthly.

The Federal Reserve Bulletin. Washington: Board of Governors of the Federal Reserve System, monthly.

Manpower Report of the President. Washington: U. S. Government Printing Office, annually.

Statistical Abstract of the United States. Washington: U. S. Department of Commerce, annually.

QUESTIONS FOR REVIEW AND DISCUSSION

1. Why is planning important?

2. Is planning a process? Why?

3. Describe the key steps in planning.

4. Many people say planning should be flexible? Why?

5. Explain the advantages and disadvantages of planning?

6. How do the "key indicators" help the manager in planning?

*"I believe that order is
better than chaos, creation
better than destruction."*

-- Kenneth Clark

ORGANIZING IN MANAGEMENT

A. Introduction

Being able to organize is one of the key aspects of managerial responsibility. A poor organizer can cost a company many dollars and customers. Good planning is ineffective if one cannot organize the firm to carry out the plans. Therefore, a manager with the ability to organize is an important component of any successful firm.

A significant number of managers are confused over which of the principles of organizational management they should adopt. Should the organizations structure be centralized or decentralized. This dispute has developed as various firms have moved from decentralization to centralization because of increasing costs and decreasing profits.

Sears is an important example of the change from decentralization to centralization. For a long time Sears practiced decentralization in their management so that they could develop the abilities of their younger managers in stores that were located in some of the less populated areas of the nation. However, decentralization was not very successful in Sears' case. Many of their long-time customers were spending their money at other retail stores and Sears' percentage of the retail market was deteriorating. Sears proceeded to a centralized organization because they felt that central management can better interpret the different trends in the economy and the changes in the buying habits of the consumer. Once Sears changed over, business picked up. However, can we determine that the improvement in business was because of the change to centralized management or was it just a by-product of the economy as a whole? Also, what is successful for one organization is not necessarily successful for other organizations. For some firms, centralization is the answer while for other firms decentralization is the better alternative.

B. What is organizing?
1. It is a meaningful function which determines:
    a) the various jobs or tasks to be done,
    b) putting particular jobs into departments,
    c) relations between various departments,
    d) coordinating all aspects of the organization.

C. What is organizational structure?
1. It is the order and responsibility of various types of relationships between the employees, the job, and departments within the company.

51

2. These relationships are made up of:
   a) human resources,
   b) physical resources,
   c) informational resources,
   d) financial resources.

D. Sources of authority within an organization
   1. Position – the nature of the position gives the person authority.
   2. Expertise – the knowledge and skill which is possessed by the person holding the position.
   3. Acceptance – the employee accepts the authority of the superior.

E. Differences between formal and informal organizations
   1. Formal organization – is the organizational chart which shows the formal authority relationships between superiors and subordinates within the organization.
   2. Informal organization – are the various working relationships, friendships, coffee klatches, social groups and other relationships that effect the work of the firm. The informal group leader emerges from within the group and is usually able to provide leadership for the group.

F. Differences between Line, Staff and Functional authority within the organization:
   1. Line authority – is the authority which relates directly to the activities necessary to the accomplishment of the firm's objectives. For example, in a textile manufacturing firm, the production of the fabric and the sale of the fabric are line activities. A line organization is one in which direct authority flows downward from the top levels of management to the lower management levels.
   2. Staff authority – deals with those who are not directly related to achieving the objectives of the organization. They give advice and serve as consultant to various units of the organization. For example, in a textile manufacturing firm, the textile engineer has staff authority.
   3. Functional authority – is similar to line authority but it cuts across organizational lines

in a specific area. For example, the personnel manager may have a say of who gets hired within any department.

4.

	Advantages		Disadvantages
	Line Authority		
(1)	It is simple	(1)	Lacks specialists
(2)	It is fast	(2)	Overworks some people
(3)	Responsibility is known	(3)	Depends on certain key people
(4)	Clear chain-of-command distribution of authority and responsibility on all levels	(4)	Delays can be caused if line managers wait for staff input before acting, causing a slowdown in productivity.
(5)	Unity of Command – each person in the chain of command has only one supervisor to whom he or she is accountable.		

	Staff Authority		
(1)	Expert advice is received from specialists.	(1)	Not always clear who is responsible.
(2)	Line executives can consult for another opinion.	(2)	Another level of bureaucracy has to be overcome for some activity to occur.

	Functional Authority		
(1)	One knowledgeable in a specific function makes the decisions.	(1)	Difficulty in determining which executive has authority.

(2) If set-up correctly, authority is simplified.	(2) Problem of determining responsibility.
	(3) Jealously among executives.
	(4) Can undermine the authority of the manager in the product division.

G. Relationship between Authority and Responsibility
  1. Authority - is the right to act or make decisions within certain limits.
  2. Responsibility - is a person's duty to perform an assigned task or job.
  3. Delegation - is the giving of some authority to a subordinate along with the responsibility for doing a specific job.
  4. Accountability - is a person's liability for performing assigned tasks.
  5. Span of Control - is the optimum number of people a manager can supervise in an effective manner.

H. Committee organization
  1. Is made up of various groups of individuals who share authority and responsibility.
      a. These groups are usually formed for specific purposes; developing a new product, new research, brainstorming, etc.
      b. Often represent large areas of the organization; marketing, finance, manufacturing, etc.
      c. These committees provide people from various parts of the organization to meet together on solving a specific problem.
      d. Allows for a free exchange of ideas providing one person or one small group does not dominate the committee and impose its view on the rest of the members.

I. Quality Circles
   1. Are voluntary groups of employees who meet to solve specific problems in the firm.
      a. They are made up of employees who do similar work.
      b. Management receives proposed solutions from each of the quality circles that are organized.
      c. It is hoped by management, that quality circles will serve to motivate employees to have more interest in their job and the welfare of the company as a whole.
      d. When quality circles are successful they serve to motivate workers into improving the quality of their work and help the firm improve its performance.

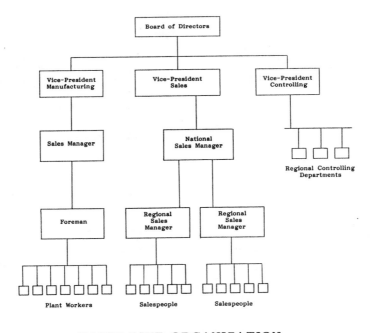

BASIC LINE ORGANIZATION

(Scaler Chain - is a downward flow of authority from top management to lower management with a decreasing rate of authority.)

J. What is Departmentalization?
    1. The grouping of job activities and functions into
        organizational units.
    2. The organizational units should be related and
        specfiic.
    3. Departmentalization may be based on technology,
        type of job, and work flow.
    4. Types of Departmentalization
        a. Functional (process) departmentalization
            groups workers according to their job
            function; e.g. marketing, production,
            accounting, etc.

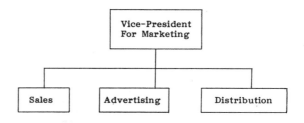

        b. Product departmentalization is grouping ac-
            cording to specific product lines. Each
            group is responsible for all aspects of
            the product whether it is manufacturing
            or marketing the product.

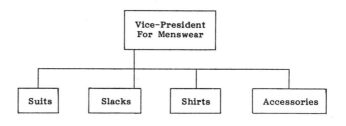

        c. Geographical departmentalization is the
            grouping of the company's product and/
            or service by location.

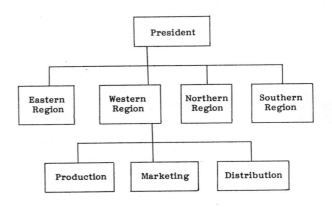

d. Customer departmentalization is based on the grouping of customers who have special requirements or characteristics.

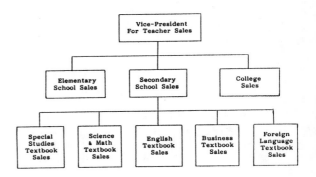

K. Centralized vs. Decentralized Authority
    1. Centralized authority - is when the majority of decision-making authority and responsibility remains within the levels of upper-management, e.g. The United States military such as Army, Navy and Air Force.
    2. Decentralized authority - is when a great deal of authority and responsibility is assigned to middle and supervisory (lower) management, e.g. General Motors, Chrysler and other American auto manufacturers are highly decentralized.

3. Advantages of Centralized and Decentralized orgazational authority.

	Centralized		Decentralized
(1)	Greater direct control to manager with most knowledge to make decisions.	(1)	Subordinates can develop the confidence and ability to make decisions.
(2)	Manager has full responsibility for the decisions.	(2)	Firm will benefit because subordinates will be able to move up within the firm and replace vacancies in higher-level management.
		(3)	Control is facilitated.

4. Computer and Centralization
    a. With the growth of computer technology it is becoming easier for firms to centralize.

L. The Functional Organizational Structure
    a) The functional organizational structure is defined as one in which there are a number of functional specialists who are responsible for supervising the activities of a single worker.
        1. Different staff departments have line authority over that particular worker.
        2. The worker and/or subordinate is accountable to all of the functional specialists.
    b) The basic idea of the functional organization was started by Frederick W. Taylor. Taylor believed that the conventional industrial foreman had so many duties that one person could not do all these satisfactorily. Therefore, he developed a structure in which each worker reported to eight foreman.

Taylor's Functional Organization

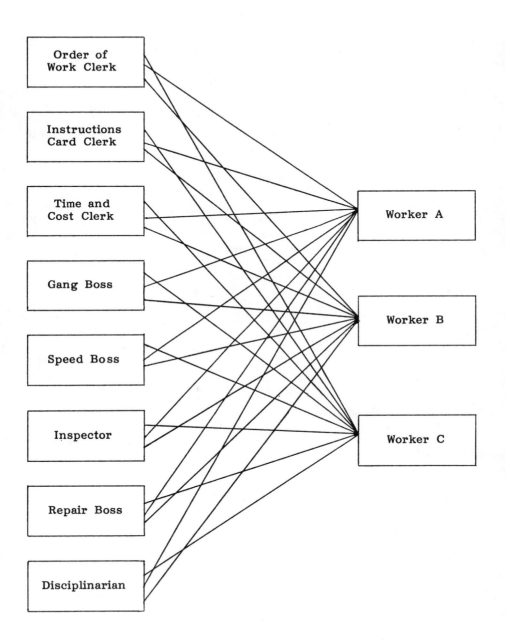

Functional Organization

Advantages	Disadvantages
(1) Permits high degree of specialization.	(1) Authority and responsibility come into conflict.
(2) Easier to fill positions because functional specialists need limited talents.	(2) At times very difficult to get specialized experts to work together in a cooperative manner.
(3) People can become expert in their particular field.	(3) Violates the principle of a person being responsible to a single authority.
(4) Provides better specialized supervision.	(4) Very difficult for a company to run smoothly when an individual is accountable to more than one person.

QUESTIONS FOR REVIEW AND DISCUSSION

1. Why is organizing important?

2. Explain organizational structure.

3. How are line, staff and functional authority different?

    a. Explain the advantages of each.

    b. Explain the disadvantages of each.

4. How is centralized authority and decentralized authority different?

    a. Under what circumstances would you favor one over the other?

*"It is hard to look up
to a leader who keeps
his ear to the ground."*

-- James H. Boren

LEADERSHIP IN MANAGEMENT

A. What is Leadership?
    1. Leadership is the ability to get people to do what the leader wants them to do. This can come about because the leader influences or inspires subordinates to achieve certain objectives.

B. Types of Influence
    1. John French, Jr. and Bertram Raven, in "The Bases of Social Power," in Cartwright, Dorwin and Zander (eds.), Group Dynamics, 2nd ed. (Evanston, Illinois: Row, Peterson & Co., 1960), 607-623 have described five main sources of leadership.
        a. Coercive Power – this is power based on fear. The fear can be either physical or psychological. Failure to comply with the desires of the superior will lead to punishment, e.g. Adolf Hitler.
        b. Reward Power – opposite of coercive power. The subordinate believes that complying with the desires of the superior will result in a positive reward, either monetary (an increase in pay), or psychological (a compliment).
        c. Legitimate Power – comes from the manager's position within the organization, e.g. The president of the company has more legitimate power than a department vice-president.
        d. Expert Power – this goes to some individual who has some special knowledge, skill or expertise which enables him to obtain the respect of peers and subordinates.
        e. Referent Power – this power is based on the subordinate's identification with the leader. The subordinates are influenced because of their admiration for the leader.
    2. It is clear the more sources of influence which a leader possesses, the more effective his leadership will be.

C. Leadership Styles
   1. Autocratic leaders
      a. Make decisions and give orders.
      b. Depend on the authority of their position to have subordinates follow them.
      c. Give little or no consideration to the opinions of their subordinates.
   2. Democratic leaders
      a. Communicates with subordinates.
      b. Seeks out the opinion's of subordinates.
      c. Decisions will most likely reflect the feelings of the group because the democratic leader accepts input from the group.
      d. Subordinates able to work more on their own because the democratic leader has confidence in them and allows them to have input in decision-making.
   3. Laissez-faire (free-rein) leaders
      a. Allows subordinates to make most of their own decisions.
      b. This type of leader gives little supervisory control.
      c. Under this type of leadership, agreement in decision-making is often difficult to get.
   4. Benevolent autocratic leaders
      a. The leader is powerful but is sincerely concerned about the welfare of his or her subordinates.
      b. McMurry, Robert N., "The Case for Benevolent Autocracy," Harvard Business Review, Vol. 36 (January-February, 1958), 82-90 favors the "benevolent autocrat" because he feels that this style is more practical because decisions are made faster and organizational democracy has not been proved.
   5. Job-centered leader
      a. Concentrates on job structure.
      b. Closely supervises subordinates.
      c. Prime desire is that all jobs are completed.
   6. Employee-centered leader
      a. Emphasizes human relations.
      b. Gives subordinates a great deal of freedom.
      c. Likert, Rensis, New Patterns of Management, New York: McGraw-Hill Book Co., 1961 came to the conclusion that

employee-centered managers were more
effective in accomplishing the objectives
of the organization than job-centered
managers.

D. Contingency Theory
    1.   Founded by Fiedler, Fred E., A Theory of Leader-
        ship Effectiveness, New York: McGraw-Hill
        Co., 1967.
    2.   Contingency Theory of leadership is based on the
        view that different leadership styles are more
        effective with different groups in different
        situations. Management action and styles de-
        pends upon the circumstances of the situation
        facing the manager.
    3.   The situation is determined by:
        a.   the size of the organization,
        b.   the manager's relation with his subordi-
            nates,
        c.   the type of job that must be performed.
    4.   Fiedler concluded that a relations oriented manager
        was very effective in leading his subordinates
        when he had a moderate amount of influence.

E. Douglas McGregor believed there are at least four variables
    involved in leadership.
    1.   The characteristics of the leader.
    2.   The attitudes and needs of the followers.
    3.   The characteristics of the organization.
    4.   The social, political and economic atmosphere.

F. Joseph Scanlon was a prize fighter, an accountant, a
    laborer in a steel mill, a local-union president, research
    director of the United Steelworkers of America, and
    finally a lecturer at M. I. T.
    1.   Scanlon's management philosophy, referred to
        as the Scanlon Plan has three broad condi-
        tions showing how all members of an orga-
        nization can contribute to its economic ef-
        fectiveness.
        a.   An established "area of collabor-
            ation," (production and screen-
            ing committees) for coordinating
            collaborative efforts through
            the organization. This is done
            without undermining collective
            bargaining or the local union.

        b. A realistic and meaningful common
            objective (the "ratio") by which
            such collaborative efforts can
            be measured.
        c. An adequate system of rewards,
            non-economic as well as eco-
            nomic, for a wide range of
            contributions to the success of
            the organization.
    2. Scanlon believed that by employing these condi-
        tions, the employees and management of an
        organization literally discover a new way of
        life. He felt that a mutual respect is de-
        veloped which helps to work out even the
        most violent disagreements. Scanlon fur-
        ther believed that every employee who
        works for a company using his plan will use
        his ingenuity to develop improvements out-
        side the limits of his own job.

Various Styles of Leadership:

The Ohio State Model*

    a. During the latter part of the 1940's there were
        attempts to analyze the behavior and style of
        various types of leaders at Ohio State Univer-
        sity.
    b. Two broad types of leadership behavior were iden-
        tified:
        1. initiating structure - referred to the
            leader's behavior in structuring the
            job or task of the subordinate and
            developing clearly-defined patterns
            of organization and communication.
        2. consideration - is the behavior of the
            leader towards the subordinate in
            the show of mutual trust and re-
            spect.

---

* See Stogdill, Ralph and Coons, Alvin E., eds. Leader Be-
    havior: Its Description and Measurement, Research
    Monograph No. 88 (Columbus, Ohio: Bureau of Busi-
    ness Research, The Ohio State University, 1957).

c. The Ohio State researchers found that the two main types of leadership behavior (initiating structure and consideration) were independent. Therefore it was possible to identify four basic styles of leadership on the Ohio State University model.
d. The focus of this model is leadership behavior.

High consideration	High consideration
Low initiating structure	High initiating structure
Low consideration	High initiating structure
Low initiating structure	Low consideration

Consideration (High / Low)

Initiating Structure (Low / High)

The Managerial Grid*

a. This is based on the leader's attitude for production and his concern for people.
b. The Managerial Grid identifies five main styles of leadership.
c. The Managerial Grid is an attitudinal model.

---

* See, Blake, R. and Mouton, Jane S. Houston: Gulf Publishing Co., 1964.

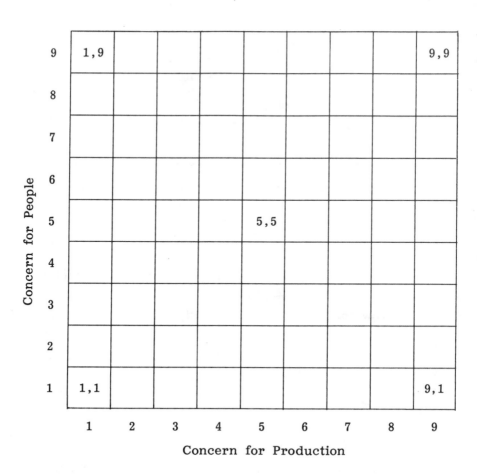

1,1 – Minimum concern for both people and pro-
      duction.
1,9 – Minimum concern for production while having
      maximum concern for people.
9,1 – Minimum concern for people, while having
      maximum concern for production.
5,5 – Moderate concern for people and moderate
      concern for production.
9,9 – Maximum concern for people and maximum
      concern for production.

Hersey and Blanchard*

    a. They look at leadership styles in terms of task be-
          havior (action taken by the leader to organize
          and define the jobs and activities of those work-
          ing under him) and relationship behavior which
          is various kinds of actions taken by the leader
          to reward people for good work, increase areas
          of communication, encourage workers and in-
          clude subordinates in various work decisions.

	Low Task → High Task	
High ↑ Relationship Behavior	Style 3 High Relationship Low Task	Style 2 High Task High Relationship
Low ↓	Style 4 Low Relationship Low Task	Style 1 High Task Low Relationship
	Low Task Behavior High	

Style 1 (high task and low relationship) – the
    leader tells the subordinates what, when
    and how they are to do things. There is
    little, if any, input from the subordinates.

Style 2 (high task and high relationship) –
    there is effective two-way communication be-
    tween the leader and the subordinates. The
    subordinates may influence the leader to
    change various plans and course of action.

* See Hersey, Paul and Blanchard, Kenneth H., Management of
    Organizational Behavior (Englewood Cliffs, N. J.:
    Prentice-Hall, 1977).

Style 3 (high relationship and low task) – the leader and the subordinates discuss ideas, problems and solutions and come to decisions together. There is a great deal of input from the followers.

Style 4 (low relationship and low task) – the subordinates make all the decisions. The subordinates who, what, when, where and how with little input from the leader unless his help and assistance is requested by the subordinates.

- - - - - - - -

G. Following are the main points of leadership as stated by Harold Geneen in his book Managing, New York: Doubleday & Co., 1984.

1. Leadership is "the single most important ingredient in business management."
2. "What you manage in business is people."
3. "Leadership...is the ability to inspire other people to work together as a team under your direction in order to attain a common objective..."
4. A leader should create an open climate stimulating growth and opportunity.
5. A leader should set an example of hard work.
6. A leader should set the goals which should be achieved.
7. The leader sets the climate over those who he leads.
8. An open atmosphere is important for successful growth.
9. Honesty is the very basis of good management.
10. "It is the duty of a leader to recognize the person who isn't doing his job and get rid of him."
11. "Firing people is always difficult. It's the moment of truth for a business leader."
12. A weak leader is ineffective. People do not wish to follow a weak leader. More respect and loyalty are given to the tough leader who is not afraid to make the tough and often unpopular decisions. However, the leader has to be perceived as decent and fair and reliable in dealing with his subordinates.
13. A leader should encourage imaginative thinking.

14. Treat subordinates with dignity and respect.
15. "Leadership is practiced not so much in words as in attitude and in actions."
16. A leader best inspires subordinates to superior performances by convincing them, by what he does and by his attitude, that he whole-heartedly supports them.
17. "A true leader has to have a genuine open-door policy so that his people are not afraid to approach him for any reason."
18. A good leader should have enough self-confidence that he can admit his mistakes and know that they will not cause his downfall.
19. A leader should avoid ruling by fear.
20. Leaders who strike fear into their subordinates turn the organization into a jungle where frightened people compete for their own personal survival instead of concentrating on what is best for the company. This is counterproductive.
21. A leader should be aware that his subordinates also have their own needs and dreams for self-fulfillment.

U.S. Marine guidebook discusses 14 character traits that every leader in the Marines or in business management should achieve.

1. Show personal integrity
2. Be knowledgeable.
3. Display courage.
4. Act in a decisive fashion.
5. Behave in a dependable manner.
6. Take the initiative
7. Be tactful.
8. Make just decisions.
9. Show your enthusiasm.
10. Develop a dignified demeanor.
11. Develop endurance.
12. Learn to be unselfish.
13. Be loyal.
14. Use good judgement.

Source: Guidebook for Marines, Marine Corps Association, Box 1775, Quantico, Va. 22134

U. S. Marines are encouraged to abide by 11 principles of intelligent leadership.

1. Take responsibility for your actions and the actions of your intelligent leadership.
2. Know yourself and seek self-improvement.
3. Set the example for those around you.
4. Develop your subordinates.
5. Ensure that a job is understood, then supervise it and carry it through to completion.
6. Know your personnel and look after their welfare.
7. Keep everyone informed.
8. Set goals that you can reach.
9. Make sound and timely decisions.
10. Know your job.
11. Develop teamwork among your subordinates.

Source: Guidebook for Marines, Marine Corps Association, Box 1775, Quantico, Va. 22134

QUESTIONS FOR REVIEW AND DISCUSSION

1. What is leadership?

2. What are the advantages and disadvantages of the following leadership styles? Which one do you favor? Why?

     a) Autocratic
     b) Democratic
     c) Laissez-faire

3. What makes a good leader?

4. According to French and Raven, discuss the five main sources of leadership as to which is most effective.

5. Describe the best leader you have ever encountered.

     a) What traits did this person possess?

     b) Why did this person impress you?

6. Why is a philosophy of management important in leadership? Or is it?

7. What is meant by the term "professional manager?"

8. Explain the difference between positive and negative leadership.

9. Discuss the basic factors of leadership.

10. How does a changing environment effect leadership?

*"It is not the size that
counts in a business. Size
is a handicap unless
efficiency goes with it."*

-- Herbert N. Casson

THE ROLE OF CONTROLLING IN MANAGEMENT

A. What is controlling?
    1. It is the process by which managers can compare performance against previously defined objectives to determine if objectives are being met.
    2. The three basic steps in the controlling process:
        a. Setting standards.
        b. Comparing results against the predetermined standards.
        c. Making corrections if there is any deviation from the standards.
    3. It is important to note that feedback is necessary to maintain control. Without feedback there cannot be any control.
    4. Controlling achieves its objectives by:
        1. Preventing some deviations before they occur.
        2. Correcting deviations as they occur.

B. Why is controlling important?
    1. Helps firm to maintain standards of performance.
    2. Holds various members of firm accountable for their performance.
    3. Helps to detect changes as they are occurring and determine if the changes are desirable.
    4. Helps to safeguard the firm's assets.
    5. Helps to standardize performance.
    6. Helps to motivate management and other employees.
    7. Helps make decentralization easier.

C. What should an effective control system possess?
    1. Information that is useful and understandable.
    2. Time conscious in that deviations are noted quickly.
    3. Flexibility to deal with varying situations and maintain control.
    4. A method which helps provide corrective action instead of just uncovering errors.

D. Financial Statements:
    1. Is an organized collection of data developed according to consistent and logical accounting procedures.
    2. Objective is to express a comprehension of various financial aspects of the company.

1. There are three main financial statements: (1) the balance sheet, (2) the income statement and (3) flow-of-funds statement.

    a. The balance sheet shows the assets, liabilities, and equity for the company at a specific date, usually at the close of the final day of the final month of the fiscal year. The balance sheet explains how the resources (assets) of the company are provided by capital from creditors (liabilities) and owners (equity).

$$\text{Assets = Liability + Capital}$$
$$\text{(owners equity)}$$

    b. The balance sheet provides a photo of the company's financial situation at the close of the accounting period. The assets or resources are shown in one column and the liabilities(debt) and equity(value) are shown in another column. Both columns should be equal to one another.

    c. When used with the income statement and other financial data, the balance sheet gives vital information on the standing of the company. Financial ratios can then be designed to provide an insight into the liquidity and profitability aspects of the firm's business. In addition, most balance sheets are comparative which means that it displays current balances as well as the balance of the previous year for each account in its columns. This enables the manager to compare the beginning and the end of year positions occurring in each account during the year. If the balance sheet is prepared correctly, it can be a fairly accurate impression of the firm's financial position at a given period in time.

    d. Balance Sheet Equation

$$\text{Total Assets = Total Liabilities + Net Worth}$$

e. The income statement:
> The income statement is a report of a company's activities during a particular fiscal period, usually one year or less. For the period in question, the income statement shows the revenues and expenses of the company, the interest and taxes, and the net income for the period. The income statement provides a summary which shows the profitability of operations over the period of time in question. It is an accounting method that shows whether the company is making a profit over the particular period of time.

E. The Flow-of-funds (sources-and-uses-of-funds) statement:
1. This statement shows the movement of funds into the company's current-asset accounts from outside sources, i.e., creditors, customers, etc. In addition, this statement shows the movement of funds used to fulfill the company's financial obligations, the retirement of stock, and/or dividends. These movements are shown for a particular time, usually for the same specific time period as the organization's income statement. Most firms put out a flow-of-funds statement as a portion of their annual reports. If they don't do this, a good analyst can develop one from the balance sheet, the income statement, and the notes to the annual report.

F. Financial statements are key tools in comprehending what happens to the organization's money as the organization conducts its business activities. When used together, the balance sheet, income statement, and flow-of-funds statement offer valuable insights into the organization's efforts to obtain liquidity and profitability.
1. Financial statements have two key uses in financial analysis.
   a. They are used to give an historical account of the organization's financial development.
   b. They are used to predict a future direction for the organization.

G. <u>Financial analysis</u> - is the process of determining the significant financial characteristics of a business firm from the accounting data. Financial statements and financial ratios are used extensively in financial analysis.

H. <u>Financial ratios</u> - is a fixed relationship in degree between two numbers.
1. Ratios are used to point out relationships that are not obvious from the raw data. Ratios are used to compare different companies in the same industry and to compare different industries in relation to their performance during various time periods.
2. Users of ratios
   a. Short-term creditors - those persons who are interested in liquidity.
   b. Long-term creditors - those who examine liquidity and profitability.
   c. Stockholders - examine liquidity, profitability and are also very concerned about the policies of the company which have an affect on the company's stock market price.

I. Major categories of financial ratios
1. Liquidity ratios - demonstrate the firm's ability to pay its debts. Two ratios are usually used to measure liquidity, (1) the current ratio and (2) the quick or acid test ratios.
   a. Current ratio is the ratio of the company's total current assets to its total current liabilities.

$$\text{Current ratio} = \frac{\text{Current assets}}{\text{Current liabilities}}$$

   A low ratio is an indicator that a firm may not be able to pay its future bills on time, particularly if conditions change thereby causing a slowdown in cash collections.
   A high ratio might show an excessive amount of current assets and may indicate a failure to properly utilize the resources of the company.
   b. The Quick ratio or acid test ratio is a stricter test of liquidity than the current ratio because inventories, which are the least liquid of current assets, are excluded from this ratio.

$$\text{Quick ratio} = \frac{\text{Cash + marketable securities + accounts receivable}}{\text{Current liabilities}}$$

This ratio indicates the ability of the company to pay its obligations without relying on the sale and collection of inventories.

A low ratio usually indicates possible problems in the prompt payment of future bills.

A high ratio could indicate that the firm is ensuring sufficient liquidity.

This calculation takes into account that inventories may not be sold.

The rule-of-thumb for approximately $1.00 in current liabilities is $1.00 in quick assets.

2. Profitability ratios:

   a. Net income to revenue – demonstrates a common percentage for indicating how profitable a company is.

$$\text{Percent profitability} = \frac{\text{Net income}}{\text{Total revenue}} \times 100$$

J. Net profits to assets – this shows that the most efficiently used assets will most likely yield the largest profits.

$$\% \text{ return on assets} = \frac{\text{Net income (from income statements)}}{\text{Total assets (from balance sheet)}} \times 100$$

K. Net profit to equity –

$$\% \text{ return on equity} = \frac{\text{Net income (from income statement)}}{\text{Average stockholders' equity (from balance sheet)}} \times 100$$

L. Earnings per share – is helpful in indicating the value of a company's stock.

$$\text{Earnings per share (EPS)} = \frac{\text{Net income (from income statement)}}{\text{Number of common shares outstanding}}$$

M. 1. Return on Investment Ratio (ROI) – is the key indicator of profitability for a firm. It matches operating profits with the assets available to earn a return.

   The firms that are efficiently using their assets will have a relatively high return, those with less efficiency will have a lower return.

$$\% \text{ of ROI} = \frac{\text{Net Profit}}{\text{Owner's Equity}}$$

M. 2. Return on Assets Ratio is a measure of earnings after taxes achieved by the firm as compared to the firm's resources.

$$\text{Return on Assets} = \frac{\text{Earnings After Taxes}}{\text{Total Firm's Assets}}$$

N. Return of Equity ratio – is used to measure the profitability of the firm. It is useful in determining the ability of the firm's management to realize a sufficient return on the capital invested by the owners of the firm.

$$\text{Return on Equity} = \frac{\text{Net Income After Taxes}}{\text{Owner's Equity}}$$

O. Earning Power ratio – is a measure of the after tax return achieved by the firm compared to the firm's resources. This ratio links after tax profits to the book value of the assets. If a firm is using its assets in an efficient manner, it will have a high earning power when compared with similar firms.

$$\text{EPR} = \frac{\text{After Tax Profits}}{\text{Book Value of Assets}}$$

P. Leverage ratio – show the relationships between the company's funds as supplied by the ownership and the firm's funds supplied by different creditors. The greater the firm's funds supplied by its creditors, the more leverage an organization has.

As a general rule, a firm should use leverage (borrowing) to the extent that borrowed money can be used to generate additional profit without a large amount of the firm's ownership being taken over by creditors.
1. Key leverage ratio
   a. $\text{Debt ratio} = \dfrac{\text{total firm's debt}}{\text{total firm's assets}}$

   Debt ratio gives the percentage of the firm's assets provided by the firm's creditors.

Q. Financial Norms:
   Five guidelines are usually used in determining financial norms.
   a. Industry norms – where a firm's financial ratios are compared with other firms in the same industry.

b. Similar firms - when a firm is compared with smaller type firms in the same industry, one can get an idea of how the firm is doing.

c. Historical comparison - the firm's performance is compared with its performance in the past.

d. Future expectancy - where past forecasts are compared as norms in the present to determine if various expectations have been achieved or have not.

e. Common sense - where the manager uses his experience, knowledge and subjective judgement.

R. Working Capital:
1. The working capital of a firm can be viewed as being comprised of two parts:
   a. Permanent working capital - these funds represent the current assets required on a continuing basis over the entire fiscal year. It represents the amount of cash receivables, and minimum inventory to carry on operations at any time.
   b. Valuable working capital - represent additional assets needed at different times during the fiscal year; added inventory must be maintained to support peak selling periods; receivables increase and should be financed following periods of high sales; and extra cash may be needed to pay for an increase in supplies preceding a period of much business activity.
2. A company's requirements for working capital are affected by four chief factors:
   a. Sales volume - different amounts of cash, receivables and inventory are needed at various sales levels.
   b. Seasonal and cyclical factors - cash, receivables and inventory should be available on a temporary basis to meet factors that are primarily seasonal or cyclical. e.g. textile industry.

      c.   Technological factors – a level of inventory is necessary to support new productive capacity of a firm. e.g. computer industry.

      d.   Company policy – some company policies tie up working capital while other policies free it.

S. Management of Current Assets

    1.   This involves two processes

      a.   Forecasting needed funds – changes in the company's operations can have almost immediate effect on the working capital needed.

      b.   Acquiring funds – once the needs have been estimated, the manager should acquire the needed funds from the best source possible, and at the lowest cost for the specific time period involves.

T. Management of Working Capital

    1.   This is the chief means of achieving the company's objective of having a satisfactory amount of liquidity. This requires monitoring the amounts of cash, receivables and inventory; and knowing the percentage of funds in current accounts.

    2.   To determine the level of working capital needed by a company, some factors should be included:

      a)   Size of the firm – a small firm may use extra current assets as a cushion against cash-flow interruptions. Large firms with access to many sources of funds may need less working capital.

      b)   The firm's activities – if a firm must keep a large amount of inventory or sell on easy credit terms, it will have a greater need for working capital than firms which provide a service or make cash sales.

      c)   Availability of credit – a company with easy access to credit from the banks will need less working capital than a company without easy access to credit.

      d)   Firm's attitude toward profits – because all funds have a cost, a relatively large amount of current assets tends to reduce the firm's profits.

e) Firm's attitude toward risk - the larger
the volume of working capital a
firm possesses, especially cash and
marketable securities, the lesser
the risk of liquidity problems.
3. In determining the proper amount of working capital that a firm needs, various studies have in-
dicated that the most successful firms usually
retain more than adequate amounts of working
capital.

U. The Gantt Chart

This is a production-control device. In this chart,
the available amount of time for each part of the production process is broken down by hours. Each job is
then determined for each division. The Gantt chart
also shows how much time it actualy took to do the job.
In this way, the person in charge of scheduling in the
production process can observe if the planning is sufficient and can make corrections when necessary.

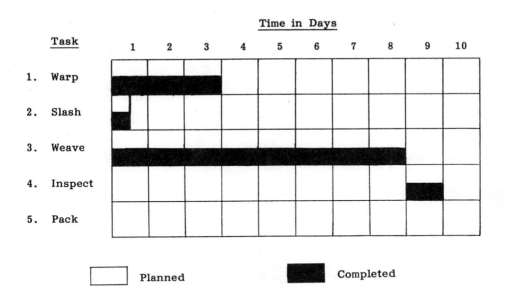

* For an excellent work dealing with Financial Analysis, Profit
Planning and Working-Capital and Cash Management; see
John J. Hampton, Financial Decision-Making, Reston, Virgin-
ia, Reston Publishing Co., 1976.

In this Gantt chart, the tasks which are necessary to produce fabric have been set out. The blocks show what tasks are scheduled to be done each day. The area filled in shows the tasks which have been completed and the length of time needed for completion.

V. PERT (Project Evaluation and Review Technique)
    1. PERT is a method of scheduling that uses network diagrams to facilitate and coordinate complex methods of production.
    2. The PERT chart helps the manager organize what should be produced when and how long it is necessary to complete each process.
        a. The manager lists each step in the process and how long it would take to complete each step.
        b. The manager then arranges the steps in the order necessary for completion.
        c. The manager then draws a diagram showing how each step is related to the other.
        d. One set of steps is the critical path. A critical path in a PERT chart is a series of operations that takes the greatest length of time to complete, provided there isn't any waste of time.
            1) The operations in the critical path are the ones in which time limits are the most important.
            2) A delay in any operation in the critical path delays the entire production process.
    3. PERT charts are used on such jobs as the building of large office and/or residential buildings.
    4. PERT charts, at times, have thousands of steps covering many months (and at times, years) of production. Presently, computers are replacing individuals in developing complex PERT charts.

QUESTIONS FOR REVIEW AND DISCUSSION

1. What is controlling?

2. Why is feedback necessary for successful controlling?

3. Explain the aspects of an effective control system.

4. Explain the three main financial statements.

5. Explain the importance of the following ratios:

    a. Current ratio

    b. Quick ratio

    c. Return on investment ratio

    d. Debt ratio.

6. How are a company's requirements for working capital affected by:

    a. Sales volume

    b. Seasonal and cyclical factors

    c. Technological factors

    d. Company policy.

*"There can be no job security
or opportunity for advancement
for the employees of a company
that isn't able to earn a profit."*

*-- Philip Murray
(labor leader)*

MANAGEMENT AND LABOR

A. What is a labor union?
   1. A labor union is when a group of workers join to-
      gether to strive for common goals, e.g. employ-
      ment security, better wages, improved benefits
      and better working conditions.

B. Differences between Craft Unions and Industrial Unions.
   1. A Craft Union is made up of skilled workers from
      the same trade, e.g. machinists and carpenters.
   2. An Industrial Union is made up of workers belong-
      ing to the same industry, e.g. auto unions and
      United Mineworkers.

C. Development of Unionism in The United States.
   1. Unionism began in the 1790's. Local groups of
      skilled workers in a particular craft joined to
      fight the division of labor and unfair hiring
      practices. To save money, employers divided
      skilled workers into teams to do only parts of
      jobs and hired women and children at extreme-
      ly low wages to do other jobs. Most of the
      early unions disbanded after their demands
      were generally fulfilled.
   2. From the 1820s to the 1850s skilled workers such
      as carpenters and printers formed citywide
      craft unions. Some local unions were able to
      form nationwide associations. However, be-
      cause of the poor communication at this time,
      nationwide unions did not flourish. Because of
      poor economic conditions in the country, many
      unions went out of existence in the late 1830s,
      but were revived in the 1840s and 1850s as the
      economy improved. However, blacks and wo-
      men were not allowed to join craft unions.
   3. The common law tradition carried to the U.S. from
      England held illegal the combining of men into
      a union, as well as the combining of businesses
      into a monopoly. In the early 19th century,
      most judges followed this line of reasoning.
      However, some of the unionists defied the
      courts and continued to strike, boycott, and
      demand (and sometimes obtain) collective bar-
      gaining rights. One important advance came
      in 1842, when the Massachusetts State Supreme
      Court declared it legal for men to organize into

a union and even to go out on strike for a
closed shop.
  a) Many American workes felt they should
     be organized because:
        1) Poor working conditions,
           unsanitary and unsafe.
        2) Low pay.
        3) Long hours.
        4) Lack of benefits.
        5) If injured on job there was
           no compensation and
           the employee was deem-
           ed to be at fault.
        6) Workers believed that there
           was strength in num-
           bers.
  b) Difficulties in organizing American
     labor
        1) Problems of leadership.
        2) Public against it.
        3) Immigrants eager for work.
        4) Blacks working for low
           wages.
        5) Different groups in labor
           force were antagonistic
           to each other.
        6) Child labor.
        7) Women workers.
        8) Lockout.
        9) Blacklists.
       10) Culture of various areas of
           country (e.g. South)
           was strongly against
           unionism.
       11) Courts viewed with dis-
           favor the growth of
           unionism.
       12) The traditional Protestants
           establishment viewed
           unionism as a product
           of immigrant groups.
4. During the first decades of the 19th century most
   of the small local unions were too weak to try
   militant action. Instead, they concentrated on
   mutual insurance schemes to provide members
   with sickness and death benefits. Moreover,
   many working class leaders felt that the only
   way to improve labor's position was through
   political action, not union organization. This

group favored a public school system, free public land for the pioneer, and an end to the imprisonment of debtors. Education and the opportunity to acquire land would, they believed, make labor free.

5. Between 1820 and 1860, as the Industrial Revolution advanced, the number of factory workers almost quadrupled. The small local unions also grew larger, uniting in city associations and national craft unions. The panic of 1837 and the eight year depression that followed caused the dissolution of many of these unions. However, with the return to prosperity, the organization of unions again progressed. Between five and ten national unions were in existence by the outbreak of the Civil War in 1861.

6. During the Civil War, there was a large demand for labor. This helped increase union membership. Many local unions and a minimum of ten additional national unions were founded. Among them was the first of the Big Four railroad unions, the Brotherhood of Locomotive Engineers (1863). But the Panic of 1873 and the following depression caused the union movement in The United States to become weaker.

7. <u>Knights of Labor</u>
   a. This union was founded in 1869 by Uriah S. Stephens.
   b. Its leader was Terrence V. Powderly.
   c. Organized on a national basis; with all workers invited to join its local lodges. Skilled and unskilled workers were invited to join.
   d. Demands of the Knights of Labor were considered to be extreme
      1) Abolition of Child Labor.
      2) Temperance.
      3) Equal pay for men and women.
      4) Establishment of cooperatively owned industrial plants.
      5) Eight-hour day.
      6) Taxes on incomes and inheritances.
      7) Workmen's compensation for industrial injuries.
      8) Postal savings banks.
      9) Government ownership of public utilities.

e. The Knights of Labor failed due to factional fights within the organization and a series of unsuccessful strikes. The chief one was the Haymarket Affair in 1886. Some maverick unions went on strike for an eight-hour day. They were joined by anarchists who hoped thereby to spread their gospel of violence. Soon Chicago was torn by clashes between strikers, strikebreakers and police. It was to protest the shooting of four strikers by police that the anarchists called a rally in Haymarket Square on May 4, 1886. When police arrived, an unknown person threw a bomb. The explosion and the rioting which then followed resulted in the death of twelve people and the wounding of many more.

f. Eight leading anarchists went on trial for murder. The Haymarket Affair was a very emotional issue at the time. The Illinois Attorney demanded, "Convict these men, make examples of them, hang them, and you save our institutions." The judge distorted the law when he was charging the jury. Influenced by the mass hysteria of the time, the jury condemned seven of the anarchists to death. Organized labor rejected the anarchists but it was too late in order to turn back the roaring tide of public opinion which, at that time, was strongly anti-labor and anti-union. Eventually the anarchists sentenced to death were given clemency by Governor Altgeld of Illinois.

g. Shrinking to less than 100,000 members by 1890, the Knights of Labor disappeared in the late 1890's.

8. American Federation of Labor (1886)

a. One of the main reasons for the demise of the Knights of Labor was its failure to get strong support from the established craft unions. A number of these unions formed a national organization of their own in 1881. Reorganized as the American Federation of Labor in

96

1886, it put its primary stress on realistic and reasonable union objectives.
   1) Only skilled workers--divided into craft groups.
   2) Samual Gompers was its president from 1886-1924.
   3) Eight-hour day.
   4) Higher wages and better working conditions.
   b. The A. F. of L. grew slowly in its early years. However, after 1898 membership climbed rapidly to a total of e.g. 550,000 members in 1900. A great upsurge in union membership brought the total to 1,675,000 members in 1905, to 2,370,000 members in 1917 and with World War I over, there was another step forward to over 4,000,000 in 1920. By 1920, about 75% of all union workers belonged to the A. F. of L.

9. <u>Congress of Industrial Organizations (C.I.O.) - 1935</u>
   a. Formed in 1935 under the leadership of John L. Lewis.
   b. Unskilled and skilled workers could belong to this union. This was different from the A. F. of L. where only skilled workers could belong.

10. <u>A. F. of L.-C.I.O. (1955)</u>
   a. The A. F. of L. and the C.I.O. were rivals until 1955 when they joined together in order to achieve gains for labor.
   b. George Meany became the leader of the AFL-CIO.
   c. Approximately one-half of the nearly 200 unions in The United States belong to AFL-CIO.

11. <u>Key legislation in the American labor movement</u>
   a. Clayton Act (1914)
      1) Called the Magna Carta of labor for it specifically exempted unions from the operation of the anti-trust laws.
      2) Defined unfair methods of competition.
   b. Adamson Act (1916)
      1) Established an eight-hour day for railroad workers.

        c.   Norris-LaGuardia Act (1932)
              1)   Limited the use of court injunctions against union striking, picketing, boycotting.
              2)   Outlawed yellow-dog contracts.

D. National Labor Relations Act (Wagner-Connery Act) - 1935
     1)   Gave legal recognition to labor unions.
     2)   Created National Labor Relations Board.
     3)   Protected workers against certain employer practices which hereafter would be considered illegal; such practices included discharging union organizers and interfering with the organizing of workers.
     4)   It held as legal secret elections of the workers in a plant, factory or store to determine which union was to be recognized as the collective bargaining agent for the workers.
     5)   Guaranteed labor the right to bargain collectively.
     6)   This act outlawed the company union.

E. Fair Labor Standards Act (1938)
     1)   Federal law which regulated women and children's work.
     2)   Regulated work performed at home.
     3)   Set minimum wages (at that time it was $0.25 per hour).
     4)   Made overtime rates compulsory.

F. Fair Employment Practices Committee (FEPC)
     1)   During World War II this committee was formed to protect workers from discrimination because of race, color, or creed. A bill to make the FEPC permanent was advocated by both Republican and Democratic parties in 1944, but when such a measure was introduced in Congress during 1945 it was talked to death by a filibuster of southern congressman.

G. Taft-Hartley Act (1947)
     1)   Reaffirmed right of workers to organize and bargain collectively.
     2)   Prohibited unions from committing unfair labor practices such as
              a)   refusing to bargain collectively with employers
              b)   jurisdictional strikes
              c)   featherbedding

> > d) violating the term's of a union's con-
> > tract
> > e) secondary boycotts (sympathy strikes).
> 3) Unions must file financial reports with the Secretary of Labor and union officials must sign statements that they are not members of the Communist party.
> 4) Unions can't contribute to help the election campaigns of candidates for Federal office.
> 5) Prohibited welfare funds contributed by the employer unless the employer has an equal voice with the union in the distribution of the funds.
> 6) Provided for a 60-day cooling off period before a union could go out on strike. During this period, if a strike affects the national welfare (such as a railroad or a steel strike), the Federal government could secure a temporary injunction. This restricts the union from striking for an additional 80 days, during which time efforts could be made to settle the dispute peacefully.
> 7) Allowed right to work without joining a union (Section 44b).

H. The Landrum-Griffin Act (1959)
> 1) Known as labor's Bill of Rights.
> 2) Unions must file annual financial reports with the U. S. Department of Labor and such information must be made public.
> 3) Union voting must be by secret ballot.
> 4) Theft or embezzlement of union funds is a criminal offense.
> 5) Union officers must be bonded.

I. Key Labor Terms
> 1. Craft unions – consist of skilled workers in specific trades such as printers and carpenters.
> 2. Industrial unions – consists of all workers in a particular industry such as the workers in the automobile industry or the textile industry, regardless of their occupation or skills.
> 3. Jurisdictional strikes – resulting from disputes between two unions over who will represent a particular group of workers.
> 4. Closed shop – is one in which every eligible worker in a shop must belong to the union. In addition the employer can only hire union members. This was forbidden by the Taft-Hartley Act.

5. Open shop - is a shop in which joining the union is voluntary.
6. Union shop - an employer can hire any person he wishes but the new worker must join the union within a specific period of time.
7. Agency shop - is one in which the employees do not have to join the union, but they must pay to the union a fee which is equal to union dues.
8. Right-to-work laws - are state laws which forbid compulsory union membership.
9. Featherbedding - workers get paid for work not done such as the fireman on the railroad.
10. Secondary boycott - work stoppage in order to force an employer to stop using the product of another company presently involved in a labor dispute.
11. Yellow-dog contract - an applicant for a job, signs a statement agreeing that he is not a member of a union and will not join a union while working for the company.

J. Management and Unions
1. Management is usually against unions because of self-interest. They resent a reduction in their authority.
2. Unionism makes the manager's job more difficult by increasing the amount of people whose approval must be received for a particular decision, and by presenting the risk that approval may not be received.
3. Middle managers can be removed from their position but management cannot fire the union or its officials.
4. Unionism increases the number of pressures that management must confront. The manager is caught between organized workers' demand for higher wages, customers for low prices and the stockholders and board of directors for larger profits.
5. Most managers believe that unions, by limiting managerial initiative and discretion, hits directly at the roots of economic progress and rising national income. Therefore, they believe that unionism tends over the long-run to lessen rather than increase the real income of the working class.
6. Most union leaders believe that they are assisting their members in achieving improvements in wages, benefits, and working conditions and are helping to achieve social progress.

7. Managers and Union leaders also have differing outlooks because of their different personal background and experience. Two-thirds of top management officials in American corporations come from business and professional families. Three-quarters of top management have been to college. Only a small percentage have engaged in manual labor at any stage in their careers.
8. Day to day problems confronted by the factory workers are something that most managers have read about in college textbooks, but have not experienced first-hand.
9. In contrast is the background of the union official, almost always a former worker, who is short on formal training but has much experience as a factory worker. Thus, it is not surprising that management and unions look at industry differently and have differing theories on personnel policy.
10. Unionism compels "management by policy" rather than by impromptu decisions.

K. Determining Labor-Management Disputes
1. Collective bargaining - is a process of negotiation between management and union representatives for the purpose of arriving at mutually acceptable pay, benefits and working conditions for the employees.
2. Mediation - is the process of bringing in an impartial third party, called an arbitrator, into a union-management dispute. The mediator stands between the conflicting parties and makes recommendations which are not binding.
3. Voluntary arbitration - is where both labor and management representatives decide to present the issues which are in dispute to an impartial third party.
4. Compulsory arbitration - is when both labor and management representatives must submit their dispute to arbitration. The third party that usually requires this is the federal government.
5. Grievance procedure - is a formal process which is part of the union contract that is used to settle differences between the union and management. Grievance handling starts when the aggrieved worker, or the union steward acting in behalf of the worker, or both the worker

101

and the steward take the grievance to the employee's immediate superior. If the grievance cannot be resolved at this level, the dispute then goes up various levels in both the union and the firm. If the dispute is not settled at the various steps, it then goes to arbitration.

6.

Union Weapons	Management-Weapons
a) Strikes - work stoppage by workers until the dispute is settled.	a) Lockout - management shuts down the firm in order to bring pressure upon the union to give in to management demands.
b) Picketing - workers parade at the entrance of the employer's place of business as a protest against management practice.	
	b) Injunction - is a court order which prohibits a particular labor practice.
c) Boycott - is an effort by the union to persuade people not to buy goods or services from a particular company.	
	c) Employer association - is a joint effort by employers to present a united front in order to deal more successfully with the labor unions.
d) Primary boycott - is one in which union members are instructed not to patronize the firm that is being boycotted.	

QUESTIONS FOR REVIEW AND DISCUSSION

1. Why were labor unions formed?

2. Why were there difficulties in organizing American labor?

3. Why did the American Federation of Labor succeed whereas The Knights of Labor failed?

4. Why did labor favor The National Labor Relations Act of 1935 while opposing The Taft-Hartley Act of 1947?

5. Explain:

   a) Craft Union

   b) Jurisdictional strikes

   c) Closed shop

   d) Union shop

   e) Agency shop

   f) Right-to-work-laws

   g) Featherbedding

   h) Collective bargaining

6. What are the main differences that confront management when dealing with unions? Can these differences be reconciled?

7. Describe the main weapons of unions in opposing management.

8. Describe the main weapons of management in opposing unions.

9. How powerful should unions become?

10. How powerful should management become?

11. What role should government play in settling labor-management disputes?

"Excellence means when a man or woman asks of himself more than others do."

-- Ortega y Gosset

A. What is Motivation?
    1. Motivation is a person's inner state which causes that person to act in such a way that strives for the accomplishment of some objective.
    2. Motivation helps to explain why people act the way they do.
    3. It is important for managers to realize how to motivate people. Good motivators can achieve a great deal through people. If a manager realizes the needs of a member of the firm, he can then do what is necessary to help that person fulfill his needs.
        a. Motivating members of the firm is the process of giving them the chance to satisfy their needs by performing in a satisfactory manner within the firm.
        b. A member of the firm who is not finding his or her needs satisfied may contribute towards the objectives of the firm in a negative way.
        c. Managers who are considered to be good motivators stress the positive aspects of a subordinate's actions instead of stressing the negative aspects of that person's actions.

B. Various management strategies involved in motivating subordinates.
    1. Good communication - subordinates who feel that they can talk to their superiors about various problems that they are confronted with, usually perform in a better fashion than if they cannot communicate in a positive way with the manager.
    2. Positive attitude towards subordinates - those managers who believe that their subordinates can and do make positive contributions to the success of the firm, help to motivate their subordinates to do a good job. A manager's attitude toward those under him comes through to the subordinates and affects their performance in either a positive or negative way, depending upon the attitude of the manager.

3. Design of job – how a manager designs a job for a specific individual has a large determination upon whether that individual performs his or her tasks well or not.
4. Job rotation – at times it is better to move people from one type of job to another to prevent them from becoming bored. Many people feel that job rotation will increase productivity.
5. Job enlargement – at times this strategy helps a worker perform in a more satisfactory manner by giving him more tasks to do. With an increase in the various tasks of the job, many workers feel that they are advancing themselves within the organization and therefore become more productive.
6. Flexitime – this motivates some workers because they are allowed to arrange the type of hours that they desire within certain parameters of the firm. By arranging their own hours some workers become motivated to perform in a more productive manner.

C. Theories of Individual Behavior
   1. Maslow's hierarchy of human needs.

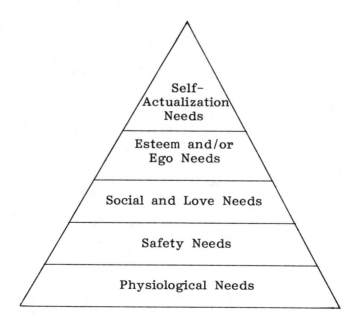

2. From lowest to the highest needs
    a. Physiological needs – the need for food,
        clothing and shelter. These needs
        come before any other needs.
    b. Safety needs – the need for safety, secur-
        ity and protection.
    c. Social and Love needs – man is a social ani-
        mal. He needs to feel wanted and loved
        by other people and the feeling of be-
        longing to a group.
    d. Esteem and Ego needs – the need for a high
        opinion of oneself. This is also the
        need to have respect and be held in
        esteem by others.
    e. Self-actualization needs – the necessity of a
        person to achieve their potential. This
        person is usually secure, self-confident,
        willing to learn from others and is
        willing to become close and have faith
        and trust in other people.
3. Maslow's theory gives managers the knowledge that
    money is not the only motivating force in get-
    ting subordinates to improve productivity.
    There are other needs, and the more a manager
    is aware of the other needs, the more effective
    he will be.

D. Kurt Lewin (1890-1947) and his field theory
    1. Lewin believed that behavior of a person is strong-
        ly influenced by his environment.
    2. Lewin's main work was A Dynamic Theory of Per-
        sonality (1935).
    3. Field Theory

$$B = f(PE)$$

B=behavior
f =function of factors
P=Person
E=Environment

Behavior = function of the factors of the per-
    son and the factors of the environment as
    they have an effect upon that person.

E. David McClelland categorized three basic needs.
    1. Need for achievement – the inner drive to achieve
        success.

2. Need for affiliation - the wish to have close inter-personal relations with other people.
3. Need for power - the desire to feel able to alter events and influence other people. They strive to reach the higher levels of power and influence in an organization.

F. Carl Rogers
1. Main work was On Becoming a Person (1961).
2. By studying all aspects of a person's self-concept, a person can understand and even predict with a large degree of accuracy, his mode of behavior.
3. Rogers strongly believed that a person's environment strongly influenced his self-concept.

G. B. F. Skinner
1. Skinner's main work was The Behavior of Organisms (1938).
2. Derived the theory of "operant behavior," in which he states that behavior is the result of various consequences.
3. Human behavior can be influenced by other people if they know what stimulus affects the person.
4. Skinner emphasized the importance of reinforcement on voluntary behavior.

H. Douglas McGregor
1. His chief work was The Human Side of Enterprise (1960).
2. Theory X and Theory Y.

Theory X	Theory Y
(1) People do not like to work and will do all that they can do to avoid it.	(1) Work is a natural act for the average worker.
(2) They do not have a sense of responsibility.	(2) Under proper conditions the average worker will seek work.
(3) They have little ambition.	(3) Workers will exercise self-direction and self-control to achieve objectives.
(4) The average worker is self-centered and does not care about the firm's goals.	

(5) The average work-
er resists any
change.
(6) The average work-
er wants job
security and
economic secur-
ity above all
else.
(7) To get the average
worker to
achieve the
firm's objec-
tives, it is
necessary to
use force, con-
trol and threats
of punishment.

(4) If workers are
committed to a
firm's objec-
tives they will
be self-moti-
vated.
(5) Workers have the
the ability for
creativity and
ingenuity in
finding solu-
tions for vari-
ous problems
that the firm
encounters.
(6) Workers are also
interested in
satisfying es-
teem and self-
actualization
needs.
(7) For the average
worker, secur-
ity is impor-
tant but it is
not the work-
ers only con-
sideration.

I. Chris Argyris
    1. <u>Immaturity-Maturity Theory</u>
        a. This theory outlines a number of changes
           that occur as a person moves from im-
           maturity to maturity such as activity,
           depth of interest, etc.
        b. Argyris comes to the conclusion that most
           firms keep their employees in a perpet-
           ual state of immaturity by discouraging
           mature behavior.

J. Victor Vroom
    1. <u>Expectancy Theory</u> that was put forward by Vroom,
        means the probability that a specific action will
        be followed by highly probable and valuable
        rewards, which in turn will lead to a large de-
        gree of job satisfaction if the rewards are con-
        sidered to be equitable.

K. Elton Mayo
1. The Hawthorne Studies were conducted by Mayo at the Western Electric Corporation in a suburb of Chicago between 1927 and 1932. The research showed a connection between the workers morale and productivity. The human relations school of management was based a great deal on the Hawthorne Studies.
2. The Hawthorne Studies under Elton Mayo came to the conclusion that better treatment of workers would increase their productivity.
3. Mayo came to the conclusion that improved productivity in both the controlled and experimental groups was because both groups received special attention from management.

L. Frederick Herzberg
1. Herzberg's main work was written with B. Mausner and B. Snyderman and called The Motivation to Work (1959).
2. Herzberg's Two Factor Theory consists of hygiene factors and motivational factors.

Hygiene Factors	Motivational Factors
(are things that would lead to job dissatisfaction).	(are things that will encourage people to achieve the firm's objectives and lead to job satisfaction).
(1) money	(1) achievement
(2) status	(2) recognition
(3) security	(3) responsibility
(4) working conditions	(4) personal growth
(5) relations with supervisors, peers and subordinates.	(5) chance for advancement.

M. There are many aspects that the manager has to consider in motivating employees. Money, of course, is very important. It is especially important when the employee receives a low wage and any decent increase in money will greatly increase the worker's productivity. However, money will not be so important if the employee is making a decent income and is interested in other things such as self-esteem, self-actualization, status, and respect.

1. The manager should be aware that not only money but psychological factors such as achievement, recognition, advancement and responsibility are also successful motivational factors in increasing productivity.

2. Each manager has to develop his own theory of motivation. However, most new managers feel that not only must they satisfy lower level needs of workers such as physiological and safety needs; but understands that many workers also feel the need to satisfy higher needs such as social, esteem and self-actualization needs.

3. In general, various theories and research are of value in helping managers develop a philosophy of how to motivate subordinates. Managers should make their objectives clear; consider objections in a sincere and fair manner and respect the views of the subordinates at all times.

QUESTIONS FOR REVIEW AND DISCUSSION

1. What is motivation?

2. Why is it important to understand motivation in order to understand the role of leadership?

3. Explain Maslow's hierarchy of needs.

   a) Which need do you consider the most important? Why?

4. Can most people attain self-actualization? Give reasons for your answer.

5. Discuss the various strategies in motivating subordinates.

   a) Which strategy is the best? Why?

   b) Which strategy is the worst? Why?

6. Explain McClelland's three basic needs.

7. How can environment affect a person's behavior?

8. How does "Theory X" differ from "Theory Y"?

   a) Which theory do you think is correct? Why?

9. How did "The Hawthorne Studies" affect ideas on productivity?

10. Why is Herzberg's "Hygiene-Motivation Theory" useful?

11. What is the best position to assume in motivating people at work?

*"He who will not reason, is
a bigot; he who cannot is
a fool; and he who dares
not is a slave."*

-- Sir William Drummond

DECISION-MAKING IN MANAGEMENT

A. What is decision-making?
   1. Decision-making deals with management's role in making a choice from among two or more alternatives in a particular situation.
   2. Decision Tree is a graphic tree-like model of a sequence of alternative decisions to be chosen and the possible results of each choice.
   3. Problem
      a. Is a chance from what normally happens.
      b. Difference between what should be happening and what is actually occurring.

B. Four Aspects of Decision-making
   1. Search
      a. What should we do?
      b. What challenges do we face?
   2. Analysis
      a. How can we use the resources that are available?
      b. How can we take advantage of the situations we face?
   3. Evaluation
      a. How much does it cost to do this?
      b. Will we benefit from doing this?
      c. How much will we gain from doing this?
   4. Commitment
      a. What choice should we take?
      b. How can we do the job best?

C. Types of Decisions
   1. Institutional decisions
      a. Deal with long-term planning.
      b. Development of organizational policy.
      c. Top managements is responsible for most institutional decisions.
   2. Managerial decisions
      a. Coordinate the main aspects of the organization.
      b. Controls the way supervisory personnel carry out their duties.
      c. Middle management is responsible for these decisions.
   3. Technical decisions
      a. Deals mainly with the actual production and/or service of the organization.

117

            b. These decisions are made mostly by super-
                visory management.
        4. Organizational decisions
            a. Those decisions a manager makes in his or
                her official role as an employee of the
                business organization.
        5. Programmed decisions
            a. Those decisions that are routine, repetitive,
                common.
        6. Non-programmed decisions
            a. Those decisions that deal with unusual,
                exceptional problems.

D. Steps in decision-making
        1. Identify and define the problem.
        2. Diagnose the situation.
        3. Collect data related to the problem.
        4. Analyze the data related to the problem.
        5. Identify the various resources available to help
            solve the problem.
        6. Identify the restraints that hinder the solution of
            the problem.
        7. Ascertain possible solutions in the solving of the
            problem.
        8. Development of alternative solutions.
        9. Evaluate all possible solutions.
       10. Implement the solution.
       11. Follow up.

E. Various aspects of managerial decision-making
        1. Different decisions require different degrees of
            risk, certainty and uncertainty.
            a. There is a degree of risk when the
                manager has some degree of knowl-
                edge of how a problem can be
                solved but lacks certain information
                so as to determine its certainty.
            b. Certainty is present when the manager
                believes that he knows all he can
                know about the problem and is
                sure of the solution.
            c. Uncertainty is when the manager has
                very little knowledge and is uncer-
                tain in how various solutions will
                turn out. Here we have a great
                deal of plain guessing.
        2. Different types of managers act in different ways.
            Some managers are more willing to take risks,

while others always look to make the safe decision. The kind of decisions a manager makes is
dependent a great deal upon the personality,
education and general characteristics of the
particular manager.

F. Herbert A. Simon (e.g. 1960)
    1. Developed the concept of "satisficing."
    2. Believed that lower-level workers' needs do not
        have to be satisfied 100% before other needs
        that are of a higher level tend to emerge.
    3. Firms try to "satisfice" rather than maximize profit.
        They are happy with a certain level of profit.
    4. Believed that managers also "satisfice" by looking
        only at a few alternatives rather than exploring
        all the possible alternatives. The managers
        then make their choices from the few alterna-
        tives.

G. Decision by committee or groups
    1. Many organizations favor decision-making by groups.
        a. This is strongly favored in Japan where
            under "Theory Z" workers are brought
            into decision-making.
        b. Some American companies are adopting
            "Theory Z."
        c. Strengths of group decision-making.
            1) More solutions proposed.
            2) More people satisfied with solution.
            3) Increased communication within
                company.
            4) More deliberation before coming to
                a decision.
        d. Weaknesses of group decision-making.
            1) Many compromises.
            2) Slower decision-making.
            3) Blaming others - "passing the buck."
            4) Some people don't perform well in
                groups and are dominated by
                others.

QUESTIONS FOR REVIEW AND DISCUSSION

1. Why is it said that decision-making is a never ending task for an executive?

2. What is decision-making?

3. Explain the key steps in decision-making.

4. Why do some organizations favor decision-making by groups?

5. Explain the strengths and weaknesses of decision-making by groups.

6. What are the different types of decisions?

7. Which kind of decision-making do you favor; individual or group decision-making? Why?

"What the heck is
quantitative techniques."

-- a former student

QUANTITATIVE TECHNIQUES IN MANAGEMENT
DECISION-MAKING

A. Forecasting
  1. Main purpose of forecasting is to predict future demand for an organization's goods and/or services and future trends. Forecasting helps the company establish objectives and make adjustments within their plans.
  2. Forecasting effects
      a. Production planning.
      b. Capital budgeting.
      c. Staffing needs.
      d. Investing requirements.
  3. Three types of forecasts used by business organizations.
      a. Long-range forecast – deals with an organization's long-term (over one year) planning.
      b. Short-range forecast – deals with an organizations immediate (less than one year) needs.
      c. Rolling forecast – requires a constant updating during the process of planning.
  4. Forecasting methods
      a. Quantitative methods – predicts future demand by using statistical techniques, econometrics and mathematical programming.
      b. Qualitative methods – is subjective prediction of future demand such as surveys, polls and predictions of various experts and executives.
  5. External forecasting
      a. Is a systematic evaluation of events in which the firm has little or no control.
      b. Some methods of external forecasting are sales forecasting, economic forecasting and predicting political events and its effect on the firm.
  6. Internal forecasting is when the firm analyzes its resources both human and physical.
  7. The quantitative approach to forecasting was derived from operations research which was developed by the British in the midst of World War II. A select group of scientists were

123

instructed to solve a number of assorted, complex problems faced by the military. One of the chief problems was determining the best size for escorting convoys across the Atlantic Ocean. The scientist faced two major constraints: (1) shipping losses had to be kept at as low a level as possible and (2) determining the minimum number of escort vessels needed to successfully complete the mission with the least losses of ships. The scientists found that large convoys having an equal number of escort vessels and smaller convoys, reduced shipping losses.

   a. In present day management, operations research is applied to complete the major part of systems instead of individual problems as previously stated. It also depends to a great extent on mathematical models (a mathematical model is the using of mathematics to represent the system being studied).
   b. Polls
      1. Used to get subjective information.
      2. Helps to analyze future economic conditions.
      3. Helps to determine attitudes towards a product or company.
      4. Polls are very useful in sales management because they can help plan future sales.
   c. Informal forecasting
      1. Exchange of information between executives of different companies.
      2. Survey trade publications.
      3. Knowledge acquired at various trade shows and exhibits.
      4. This is a very subjective method.
8. Barometric Indicators
   a. The company works in the belief that profit is related to the amount of sales, which is related to the state of the economy in the country.

b. Uses leading indicators to judge future aspects of the economy. e.g.
   1) rise or fall of stock market.
   2) rise or fall of sales.
   3) housing starts.
   4) automobile sales.
   5) retail sales.
   6) Magazines such as U. S. News and World Report and Business Week publish lists of various indicators which business can uses to predict future economic activity.
c. Different firms use various economic indicators in different ways. A company has to select from the different sets of indicators those which are most in line with what they need.

9. Econometric models
   a. This is the combination of statistics, mathematics and economics.
   b. Econometrics involves using history to predict what will happen in the future.
      e.g. If a particular item has achieved a particular amount of sales over the years, it is possible to develop a mathematical relationship between what consumers spend for that item and the amount of income they have. Once this relationship has been proved statistically, forecasting would say that since this relationship has been in effect for so many years in the past, it will probably be in effect next year.

10. Delphi forecasting
    a. Based on two main points
       (1) those who know most about a field will make better forecasts.
       (2) the combined efforts of several people is better than one.

b. Used for the predictions of success of new products, allocations for resources and developmental planning.

11. Forecasting usually involves the combination of facts and executive judgements. It is difficult to determine which one is more important than the other. Different industries, different companies within the industry, different types of managers all determine which is more important for a particular situation. However, it is safe to say that both qualitative and quantitative are very important and most companies use a combination of both.

QUESTIONS FOR REVIEW AND DISCUSSION

1. Why do firms use forecasting?

2. What are the three types of forecasts used by business organizations?

3. How is quantitative methodology different from qualitative methodology?

4. Explain

    a. Barometric indicators.

    b. Econometric models.

    c. Delphi forecasting.

*"The great creative individual
is capable of more wisdom
and virtue than collective
man ever can do."*

-- John Stuart Mill

THE MANAGEMENT OF HUMAN RESOURCES

A. Why is human resources management important?
   1. The key element of an organization is the people who work for that group.
      a. The organization runs on how the workers carry out their assigned functions in order to achieve the organization's objectives.
      b. Matching the correct person with the correct job is a vital function of the human resources department.
         1) The correct people are usually found within the firm.
         2) Human resource departments sometimes have to go outside the company.

B. Planning in the area of human resources:
   1. Planners have to determine what type of employees the firm needs and how many of each kind are necessary.

C. The process of selection:
   1. It must be generally understood that larger firms in most cases use more complex selection methods than smaller firms.
   2. Selection methods for upper-level management and technical staff jobs are generally much more complicated than the procedures for lower-level jobs.
   3. Various steps in the selection process:
      a. Recruitment
      b. Application
      c. Preliminary screening of applicants
      d. Testing
      e. Check of references
      f. Final interview
      g. Evaluation.

D. Governmental influences:
   1. The Civil Rights Act - passed in 1964 and expanded in 1972 prohibits discrimination in all types of personnel practices and policies, such as recruitment, interviewing, testing, compensation, promotion, union-management relations,

and different kinds of treatment based on race,
color, religion, sex or country of national origin.
2. The Civil Rights Act is enforced by the Equal Employment Opportunity Commission (EEOC).
3. Affirmative Action programs have been developed with the desire to increase job opportunities for minorities and women.

E. Training and Development
   1. Orientation - is the introduction of new employees or those recently moved to a different job to the newer aspects of their new job.
      a. All orientation programs should include:
        1) the firm's background
        2) introduction to coworkers
        3) various aspects of the new worker's job
        4) company policies
        5) company benefits.
   2. On-the-Job Training (OJT) is to teach the employee how to do the job while he is on the job. This is usually done under the supervision of an experienced and productive worker. On-the-Job training should include:
      a. Planning.
      b. Preparing the worker.
      c. Showing the worker the methods and various operations of the job.
      d. Observing the worker at his new job and making suggestions as necessary.
      e. Follow-up and evaluation.

F. Management Development:
   1. Management development training usually includes many activities and a variety of experiences.
      a. Types of Development
        1) On-the-Job training for managers. They learn how to manage by managing.
        2) Classroom attendance.
        3) Formal guidance from a supervisory manager, known as coaching.
        4) Seminars - both formal and informal.
        5) Staff meetings.

   6) Role playing - used in develop-
     ing human relations skills.
   7) Management games - people are
     put on teams and compete
     against each other.
   8) Sensitivity training - this is to
     develop realization of the
     effect of your actions on
     other people.
   9) Job-rotation - a manager can
     learn various things about
     the organization by moving
     from one job to another.
   10) Attend courses at local colleges.
   11) Self-development.

G. Performance Review:
  1. During a performance review the manager and the
    subordinate should discuss the quality of the
    subordinate's performance; ways to improve;
    problems that they face; and what can be done
    in the future.
  2. Some methods of performance review are:
    a. Rating scales.
    b. Management-by-objectives (MBO) forms.
      1) Some of the difficulties with MBO
       are that managers often set un-
       realistic goals that are either
       unattainable or so easy that it
       doesn't take any effort.
      2) Some managers also hold the sub-
       ordinate responsible for some-
       thing that is beyond his control.
    c. Follow-up of the performance-review.
      1) During this period of time the sub-
       ordinate is observed to form
       the basis of discussion for the
       next performance review.
    d. The great jackass fallacy.
      1) This means that subordinates know
       the difference between being
       positively motivated by man-
       agers and being manipulated
       and therefore are not fooled by
       managers who are insincere and
       try to manipulate the subordi-
       nates via a "carrot and stick"
       type reward system.

H. Compensation and employee benefits:
  1. Job evaluation - determines the salary level for various jobs by determining the nature of the job, the degree of responsibility involved on each job, the amount of education needed and the physical nature and risk involved. By comparing one job with another job within the firm a relative degree of comparable worth may be determined. However, one should understand that a job that is worth a particular amount to one company may be valued differently by another company.
  2. Direct monetary compensation.
     a. Wages or salary - the actual amount of money being paid to perform a specific job.
     b. Bonuses - some companies have plans that specifies if an individual performs successfully a specific amount of work, that individual will receive extra compensation.
     c. Profit sharing - if the firm makes a profit this is shared with the employees.
     d. Stock sharing.
  3. Indirect Compensation.
     a. This is called fringe benefits and is made up of:
        1) Retirement plans.
        2) Health plans, e.g. medical and dental plans.
        3) Life insurance plans.
        4) Sick leave.
        5) Vacations and holidays.

I. Promotion, transfers and separations.
  1. Promotions - can be based on an employee's merit, seniority, ability and sometimes nepotism and political connections.
  2. Transfers - movement from one part of the company to another job within the company. This is usually called a lateral move that may be brought about because of differences between the worker and his superior or due to boredom or a deterioration of relations between one worker and another.
  3. Separations are made up of:
     a. Resignation - voluntary leaving of firm by employee.

b. Layoffs - temporarily putting worker off job due to bad business times or plant conversion or the closing or moving of physical facilities.
c. Dismissals - a person being fired normally for poor performance but not always the case.
d. Retirements - after working for a specific number of years an employee leaves with hopefully a sufficient pension.

QUESTIONS FOR REVIEW AND DISCUSSION

1. Why is human resource management important?

2. How is government influencing human resource management?

3. What methods do company's employ to develop managers?

4. Why is the performance review important to employee development?

5. Differentiate between direct and indirect compensation.

6. Discuss the various ways in which a person is separated from a company.

7. How does a company select personnel?

"A word to the wise is not enough, if it doesn't make any sense."

--James Thurber

THE ROLE OF COMMUNICATION IN MANAGEMENT

A. Managers should understand the importance of communication. Good communication is important for successful managerial functioning. It is extremely important for managers to get their ideas across to subordinates and for their peers. If people do not understand the manager's thought, it is virtually impossible to achieve the various objectives of the firm.

B. What is communication?
   1. Communication is the process of the interchange of information and thoughts between two or more people.
   2. Communication has the purpose of:
      a. Inquiring
      b. Informing
      c. Persuading.
   3. Communication skills
      a. Speaking
      b. Reading
      c. Writing
      d. Body language.

C. Barriers to communication:
   1. Noise
   2. Emotions
   3. Language
   4. Lack of information
   5. Beliefs
   6. Poor channels
   7. Inappropriate timing
   8. Misperception
   9. Using words that have multimeaning
   10. Lack of attention
   11. Omission of details
   12. At times, too much information.

D. Keys to effective communication:
   1. Be clear
   2. Be concise
   3. Be aware of the physical and emotional atmosphere while communicating
   4. Be positive whenever possible
   5. Be careful of the timing of the communication
   6. Be a good listener
   7. Be careful
   8. Follow-up.

E. Channels of communication:
   1. Formal channels
      a. Approved by the organization
      b. Recognized methods of communication within the organization.
   2. Informal channels
      a. These are channels outside the approved channels within the company. This is known as the grapevine.
      b. Management should be aware of the grapevine and try to use it as effectively as possible.

F. Effective communication between the manager and subordinates can increase the positiveness of the atmosphere of the firm.
   1. Morale can be improved.
   2. Productivity may be increased.
   3. Good communication requires a great deal of effort but it is worth the effort if a manager wants to successfully achieve the firm's goals.

G. Formal Organization:
   1. Upward communication
      a. Ways of achieving upward communication:
         1) Open-door-policy - the superior always being ready to discuss problems with subordinates.
         2) Committees.
         3) Interviews - used in counseling, hiring and termination of employment.
         4) Grievance procedure - a means which enables employee complaints to be settled by appeals to higher levels.
         5) Suggestion system - a system of encouraging employees to communicate their ideas to their superiors.
   2. Downward communication
      a. This is the communication from the top levels to the bottom levels.
         1) Memorandums
         2) Staff releases
         3) Telephone communication
         4) Company newsletters
         5) Face-to-face discussion.

3. Cross Communication
      a. Means of Cross-communication.
          1) Newsletters
          2) Manuals
          3) Letters.

H. Informal Communication:
    1. Does not follow channels of authority.
    2. Information transmitted by informal channels of communication, e.g. "grapevine."

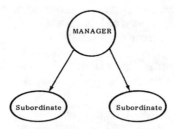

Downward Flow of Communication

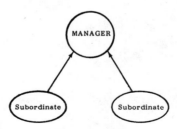

Upward Flow of Communication

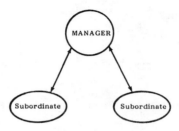

Two-way Flow of Communication

1. Why is it necessary for a manager to have good communication with subordinates?

2. What is communication?

3. What are the barriers to good communication?

4. What are the keys to good communication?

5. Many public figures are known for being good in communicating their thoughts. Give some examples of public figures who you feel to be good communicators and explain why you feel they are?

6. Give some examples of public figures who you feel are poor communicators and state why you feel they are.

*"Willful waste brings
woeful want."*

-- Thomas Fuller

A. What is production?
    1. Production is the processes and actions needed to change inputs into outputs (goods and/or services).

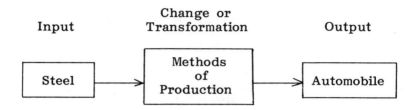

Input	Change or Transformation	Output
Steel	Methods of Production	Automobile

B. Types of production systems:
    1. Continuous flow - produces a standardized item which is carried in inventory.
    2. Intermittent flow - produces items that are made to fit the specifications of a particular customer.
        e.g. a specific style of clothing is made for a particular customer in the textile industry.

C. Coordination:
    1. Due to systems engineering and program management, the coordination of extremely complex systems is made possible.
        a. James G. March & Herbert Simon Organizations (1958) state that there are three types of coordination for production.
            1) Coordination by standardization - the setting of rules and standard operating procedures for all similar components throughout the firm.
            2) Coordination by plan - the establishing of time and program schedules connecting interrelated parts.

3) Coordination by mutual adjustment - this is the exchange of information between interrelated components of the firm.
   2. Careful and planned coordination can increase efficiency and prevent unnecessary duplication of efforts.

D. Steps in developing a system of production:
   1. Decide the product or service to be produced.
   2. Research and Development
      a. Why should it be produced?
      b. How can it be produced?
      c. How much of it should be produced?
   3. Choose the site of the plant.
      a. Closeness to market, e.g. textiles in North Carolina.
      b. Taxes, cost of materials, attitudes of community should also be considered.
   4. Design the plant so production can be developed as effectively as possible.
   5. Design the various jobs
      a. What does the job entail?
      b. What type of environment, both physical and social, is needed to perform the job as efficiently and with the best productivity possible.
   6. Methods of controlling production.
      a. Can we produce the item?
      b. How much of the item can we produce?
      c. Do we have the resources to produce the item?
   7. Quality control procedures
      a. What level of quality do we want?
      b. How often do we check quality?
      c. How do we correct deviations?
   8. Inventory control requirements
      a. How much of each item do we need?
      b. What type of system should we use?
         1) Fixed quantity system - a fixed amount is kept of each item.
         2) Fixed interval system - items are reordered at specific times.
         3) Minimum-maximum system - inventory is checked at specific times, but there is no reordering unless various items fall below a particular level.

9. Shipping
    a. Where do we store the goods?
    b. Where should the trucks receive the goods?

E. Productivity
1. Productivity is the number of man-hours needed to produce a particular number of goods.
2. During the 1970's and into the 1980's productivity had been on the decline in the United States. Many reasons for this have been put forth. Among them are:
    a. Contracts between union and labor.
    b. Change in attitude toward work.
    c. Poor supervision.
    d. Workers do not feel they have any input in the productive process.
    e. Government regulation – e.g. safety regulation through O.S.H.A.
    f. Interest in short-term profits instead of long-term planning on the part of managers in many industries, e.g. automobile industry.
    g. Less money being spent on research and development.
3. Within the last few decades there has been a tremendous increase in productivity on the part of the Japanese.
    a. William Ouichi has stated that Theory Z is the basic reason for Japan's economic success. The Theory Z approach has certain elements that might encourage productivity on the part of the Japanese worker.
        1) A lifetime guarantee of employment.
        2) Increased productivity is the result of involving workers in planning and the solving of problems through consensus.
        3) Company and personal objectives can be achieved through long-range planning.
        4) A strong bond of loyalty is developed between the workers and the employers.

     5) Jobs are rotated to relieve
       boredom and keep the
       workers interested.

4. During the years of the Reagan administration in
  The United States there have been attempts to
  increase productivity. These attempts have
  been both at the governmental level and the
  non-governmental level.

    a. Labor unions and management have
      signed contracts in which there has
      been clauses relating to increases
      in productivity.

    b. Management has included workers in
      areas of planning and decision-
      making.

    c. Due to the recession in the early 1980's
      with the increase in unemployment,
      and the loss of jobs to foreign
      industry, both workers and manage-
      ment became more aware of quality
      and productivity in order to keep
      jobs in The United States.

    d. Quite a number of American firms have
      begun a variety of programs with
      the objective of achieving improve-
      ments in quality and productivity.

    e. The Reagan administration put through
      changes in the tax laws and invest-
      ment credits with the goal of in-
      creasing productivity in the private
      sector.

    f. The National Commission on Produc-
      tivity has been established with the
      objective of studying various ways
      of increasing productivity in the
      U. S.

5. Can the United States adopt Theory Z?

    a. The United States can adopt some aspects
      of Theory Z but it should be remember-
      ed that the U. S. is a different society
      from the Japanese with a different cul-
      ture and with many different attitudes
      towards work.

      1) Within the U. S. culture there
       is still a strong desire by
       many to own their own
       business and have the
       chance of making it "on
       their own."

                    2) Many U. S. workers do not
                        wish to be tied to a firm
                        for their whole career.
                        They want to make the deci-
                        sions themselves and hope
                        eventually to move to other
                        firms for more money and
                        greater opportunity.
                    3) Many American workers are loyal
                        to their union and refuse to
                        transfer the loyalty to the
                        job.
                    4) The U. S. has the tradition of
                        being a capitalistic society
                        and has achieved the high-
                        est standard of living in
                        the world by its capitalistic
                        tradition and most of the
                        working class in the U. S.
                        is not looking to change the
                        basic system of America.

F. Information is especially important for managers of produc-
    tion.
        1. Information is the gathering of data which is
            then analyzed and then conclusions are
            drawn. It is necessary in helping the
            manager make informed decisions.
                a. Information should be relevant, of
                    good quality, of enough quanti-
                    ty and carefully prepared.
        2. A Management Information System (MIS) is a
            computer based system which has been de-
            veloped for providing data.
                a. An MIS performs seven activities:
                    1) assembles information -
                        obtains data
                    2) processes information -
                        summarizes data
                    3) analyzes information -
                        computes various types
                        of data
                    4) stores information - files
                        data
                    5) retrieves information -
                        obtains data when
                        needed

6) evaluates information –
judges if the data is of
good quality
7) output of information –
gives necessary data
when called upon.

PRODUCTION DIVISION

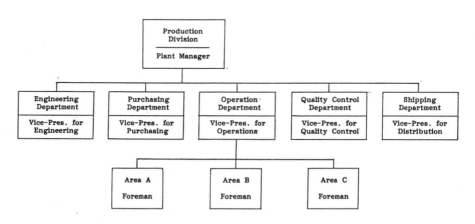

3. In the use of Management-Information-Systems,
the manager should not only rely on the
use of data, he or she should be aware
that the firm is still made up of people and
that the use of data without taking into
consideration the human element within the
firm can provide a hinderance instead of a
help to achieving the objectives of the firm.

QUESTIONS FOR REVIEW AND DISCUSSION

1. What is production?

2. Why is coordination important in the management of production?

3. Explain the steps necessary in developing a system of production.

4. What is productivity? Why has it been on the decline in the last decade in The United States?

5. Why has productivity been on the rise in Japan?

6. Can the U. S. adopt "Theory Z"? Why?

7. What is the criteria for good information?

8. Explain the key elements of a Management-Information-Systems.

*"One of the weaknesses of
our age is our apparent
inability to distinguish
our needs from our greeds."*

-- Don Robinson

THE SOCIAL RESPONSIBILITY OF MANAGEMENT

A. What is meant by social responsibility?
   1. Social responsibility means different things to different managers. Like most people, different managers have different conceptions of what the term "social responsibility" means. However, a working definition of social responsibility might be:
      a) Social responsibility is the desire of management to do the things necessary in its policies, methods, and procedures to benefit the local community and the society as a whole as they benefit their firm.

B. Should a firm be socially responsible?
   1. Most firms believe that they have social responsibilities to the rest of society. However this was not always so. Social responsibility in business has moved through three stages:
      a. Profit maximization – the only goal of a business firm is to make as much profit as possible.
      b. Trusteeship management – the firm has responsibility to other people such as vendors, employees and customers.
      c. Benefit of society management – the company had an interest in the welfare of society, not only in the benefit of the firm.
   2. Views against business performing socially responsible activities.
      a. The noted economist, Professor Milton Friedman of the University of Chicago and author of Free to Choose has taken a stand against business being involved in socially responsible activities.
         1) Dr. Friedman believes that it should be the function of government.
         2) Friedman believes that it is a conflict of interest for managers to try to achieve profit objectives and still be responsible

for improving social
welfare.

    3)   Professor Friedman takes
the position that busi-
ness will be harmed if
it has to perform so-
cially responsible deeds
which conflict with
successfully achieving
the firm's objectives.

    4)   Professor Friedman also
states that managers
who spend company
money to foster social
welfare projects, by
doing so, may be com-
mitting unethical prac-
tices, since they are
spending money which
belongs to other people.

3.   Views supporting business performing socially responsible activities;

    a.   Business is a part of the society in
which we live and therefore has to
be interested in the welfare of the
society in which it is a part.

    b.   Many people believe that business
should consider the welfare of the
society. It is not there just to
take from the society, but must
contribute to the society in which
it exists.

    c.   A good and safe society and a good
atmosphere contributes to the welfare of business, therefore, business has the obligation to try and
better society.

    d.   A business that is socially responsible
is well-respected and looked up to
by people and therefore more people want to have relations with that
firm and that in turn will increase
the firm's profits.

4.   Federal laws and controls requiring firms to have
some social responsibility:

    a)   Fair labor Standards Act (1938) -
established the first federal minimum wage at $.25 per hour,

154

prohibited many types of coercive
activities that management did.
- b) Equal Pay Act (1963)
- c) Water Quality Act (1965)
- d) Air Quality Act (1967)
- e) Noise Pollution and Abatement Act (1970)
- f) Highway Safety Act (1973)
- g) Various increases in the minimum wage
  - the hope in this is that people
  get a certain minimum amount of
  pay so that they are not taken advantage of. However, some people
  feel that a high minimum wage
  contributes to the high rate of
  teenage unemployment because em-
  ployers are often reluctant to hire
  an inexperienced, untrained teen-
  ager.
- h) OSHA - Occupational Safety and Health
  Administration - enforces various
  laws regarding the health and welfare of the worker.
- i) Department of Labor - deals with various problems faced by labor.
- j) States, cities and counties have a
  variety of labor, health and safety
  laws that force companies to have
  at least a minimum of social responsibility.
5. Sethi model of a company's social responsibility has
three steps:
- a) Fulfilling social obligations
- b) Showing social responsibility
- c) Responding to social needs.
6. Many firms now show social responsibility by:
- a) Scholarships
- b) Camps
- c) Contributions to various charities
- d) Improving the physical environment in the
  community in which they exist
- e) Cultural projects
- f) Providing summer jobs for students
- g) Providing volunteers to partake in community projects
- h) Treating employees in a fair manner
- i) Treating customers in a fair manner
- j) Producing a product or providing a service
  that society needs.

7. A company makes a large contribution to society by running its affairs in a fair and equitable manner. There isn't anything wrong in a company earning a fair profit. That is the main objective of the firm. However, if the firm earns its profit by providing a necessary and/or desired service or product and treats its employees, customers and competitors in a fair way, it is entitled to a profit and there is nothing evil or wrong with it.

QUESTIONS FOR REVIEW AND DISCUSSION

1. What is meant by social responsibility?

2. Why should a firm be socially responsible?

3. Explain the views of those who argue agaisnt a firm being socially responsible.

    a) Do you agree? Why?

    b) Do you disagree? Why?

4. How has the federal government encouraged private enterprise to be more socially responsible?

5. How have many firms shown their social responsibility?

"I'm scared!   I don't know whether the world is full of smart men bluffing ... or imbeciles who mean it."

                    -- Morris Brickman

THE MANAGEMENT OF CONFLICT

A. Conflict is a part of managerial life:
   1. All firms have some degree of conflict.
      a. Managers spend a good portion of their time in trying to resolve various forms of conflict.
      b. Conflicts can have both positive or negative results.
      c. Conflicts in companies are often the result of differences of opinion between competing groups. The groups can be competing over:
         1) financial allocations
         2) recognition
         3) salary
         4) benefits
         5) promotions
         6) philosophy
   2. Managers should be aware that in competition between groups there is healthy competition which can inspire the various groups to be more productive and there is competition which can have negative results on the various groups in particular and the firm in general.
      a. Positive competition will focus on issues rather than individual personalities and will stimulate more creativity and better ideas.
      b. Negative competition will focus on personalities rather than issues and can produce an atmosphere of fear, suspicion and lack of cooperation.

B. What managers can do in dealing with conflict:
   1. Determine what the conflict is about.
   2. After determining what the conflict is about, the manager should determine why there are differences between the individuals or the groups.
      a. Do they have different philosophies?
      b. Are they acting on differing sources of information?
      c. Is their leadership trustworthy or is the leadership using the group for totally selfish motives?

C. Warren H. Schmidt, "Conflict: A Powerful Process for (Good or Bad) Change," Management Review, December, 1974 discussed the positive and negative results of conflict.

Positive	Negative
(1) People communicate with each other.	(1) People don't communicate with each other.
(2) Issues are focused upon.	(2) Concentration on personalities instead of issues.
(3) Various opinions are exchanged.	(3) Some people refuse to discuss issues.
(4) People feel they are part of the decision-making process.	(4) Some people feel left out.
(5) People direct their efforts toward achieving the objectives of the organization.	(5) People direct their efforts on their own personal objectives instead of the organizational objectives.
(6) Cooperation in trying to solve problems.	(6) People get the feeling of "What's the use?"
	(7) Some good people leave the firm.
	(8) Lack of cooperation in solving problems.

QUESTIONS FOR REVIEW AND DISCUSSION

1. Why does conflict occur within a firm?

2. How can managers resolve conflict?

3. How can conflict have a positive effect on a company?

4. How can conflict have a negative effect on a company?

*"It is not from the
benevolence of butcher,
the brewer, or the baker
that we expect our dinner,
but from their regard to
their own interest."*

-- Adam Smith

A. What is small business?
    1. A small business is when an entrepreneur (usually he or she is the owner-manager of a small business) takes on the financial risk of starting up a business.
    2. A small business is one that is independently owned and operated and is not a major force in its industry.
        a. Capital is given to the business by one person or a small group of individuals.
        b. The size of the company is small compared to other companies in the industry.
    3. A small business is one whose activities are usually retail or wholesale, construction and production.

B. Why people go into small business:
    1. Independence.
    2. Chance for big profits.
    3. Chance to develop their own ideas.
    4. Self-actualization.

C. What type of person is the entrepreneur?
    1. Self-motivated.
    2. Commitment to the enterprise.
    3. A strong sense of responsibility.
    4. Self-disciplined.
    5. Willingness to work very hard.
    6. Desire to be independent.
    7. Perseverance.
    8. Does not get discouraged easily.
    9. Willing to take calculated risks.
    10. An action-oriented individual.
    11. A strong desire to succeed.
    12. Sets objectives and wishes to achieve them.
    13. A high degree of energy,

D. Important terms:
    1. Franchise - the right to use an established name to sell a product and/or service. e.g. McDonald's a fast-food chain and NAPA which is an auto parts franchise.
    2. Venture Capitalist - a person who looks for new areas in which to invest money.

3. Small Business Administration (SBA) - an agency of the federal government which helps small businesses with loans, training, publications and additional help for minority businesses.

E. What type of management should a small business have?
   1. A small business manager should understand the principle of management the same as a manager in a big firm. However, the small business manager has a greater variety of responsibilities and usually his own capital tied up in the venture. Therefore, the small business manager has to be adept at a variety of managerial endeavors but must not be afraid to call upon expert help when he is faced with a situation outside his area of knowledge.

F. Basic Plan for starting a new business (Based on pamphlets put out by the Small Business Administration).
   1. Determine what kind of business you are in.
   2. What goods and services do you provide?
   3. Determine where your market is.
      a) Who will buy your product or service?
      b) Why will they buy it?
   4. Determine the competition you will encounter.
   5. Develop a sales strategy.
   6. Develop plans of production, construction servicing and merchandising.
   7. Develop plans for financial analysis and data.
   8. How will the business be organized and what kind of personnel will you employ?
   9. Cash flow and break-even analysis.
   10. A system of management controls must be developed.
   11. A method of revising plans to fit changing conditions should be designed.
   12. Putting plans into action.

G. Planning is very important in starting a new business. It should be noted that over 250,000 new businesses are started in the U. S. each year and about 75% of these businesses fail within the first five years.
   1. If people would plan more carefully there would probably be less business failures.

H. Advantages and disadvantages of a small business.

Advantages	Disadvantages
(1) Can respond to change quickly.	(1) Lack of expertise in vital areas of management.
(2) Decisions are made faster.	(2) Lack of capital and various problems because of difficulty in attracting adequate financing.
(3) Ideas can be tried more quickly.	
(4) Closer personal relationship with customers.	
(5) Closer personal relationship with suppliers.	(3) Problems in getting qualified employees.
(6) A successful business venture brings about a great deal of self-actualization to the entrepreneur.	(4) The owner-manager can work extremely hard and still lose in the end.
	(5) High degree of risk.

I. Franchising
   "Buying a franchise is probably the quickest, easiest, and most successful way of becoming an entrepreneur."

Colonel Sanders - Founder of
Kentucky Fried Chicken

1. What is a franchise?
   a. A franchise is the right to use an established name (e.g. Wendy's) or idea to sell particular products and/or services. The chief aim of a franchise is to facilitate the distribution of the particular product and/or service.
      1) Franchises generally do business under the same name and usually have similar store layouts, similar prices, and similar policies in conducting the operation of their business (e.g. McDonald's, Wendy's, Burger-King, etc.).

2. Advantages for a small entrepreneur to obtain a franchise:
    a. Immediate use of a business organization with an established and hopefully a good reputation.
    b. The new owner of a franchise usually receives training in the operation of the business and is then provided help on a continuing basis.
    c. The new owner also receives benefits of national advertising and promotional campaigns.
    d. Franchisors in many cases, provide financial support for the new owner or can help raise capital because of their reputation.
    e. Franchisors provide known products and established methods of doing business which avoid many errors a new owner might make.
3. Costs of obtaining a franchise:
    a. <u>Payment of an initial fee</u> - the amount of money paid is dependent upon the nature and reputation of the particular franchise. For example, McDonald's charges a much higher initial fee than many other franchisors because of its known reputation for efficiency and quality.
    b. The franchisee may also have to purchase in his fee:
        1) specific equipment
        2) goodwill
        3) other tangible assets the franchisor deems appropriate.
    c. Many franchisors require the franchises to pay a continuous franchise service fee based on a percentage of gross sales or some other particular measure. This is done to pay for such items as advertising, supplies and services.
    d. Rules and regulations a franchise must abide by:
        1) Methods of doing business.
        2) Quality of product and/or service.

           3)   Design of place of business
                   (e.g. Pizza Hut, McDonald's).
           4)   How the business may be sold.

4.   Evaluation of a franchise opportunity:
      a.   Research all information possible about the company.
      b.   Evaluate all aspects of the business.
      c.   Get help from a variety of professionals, e.g. accountants, lawyers, analysts, etc.
      d.   Consult with others who have the franchise and others who are in similar types of business.
      e.   It is highly recommended that you deal with a franchise that has an established and reputable name.

5.   Things to beware of in purchasing a franchise:
      a.   Fast-talking con artists.
      b.   Pie-in-the-sky schemes.
      c.   Shortcuts to fortune.

6.   Future of franchising:
      a.   International markets will be opened to franchises.
      b.   New Marketing methods.
      c.   New legislation to enhance opportunities in international franchising.
      d.   New methods of sales promotion.
      e.   New types of advertising to appeal to the international arena.

7.   Franchising may be a quick way for a small entrepreneur to get into a business but it still requires perseverance, research, determination, and plain old-fashioned hard work.

      Some people do not go into franchising because they feel that they do not have the freedom to be as creative as they wish because of the restrictions of the franchisor. However, a franchise does provide the entrepreneur with the opportunity to achieve the profits in conducting the business, any additional profit due to increased value when selling the business, and an opportunity to improve the nature and quality of the business.

QUESTIONS FOR REVIEW AND DISCUSSION

1. What is a small business?

2. Why do people go into small businesses?

3. What type of person is an entrepreneur?

4. How does the Small Business Administration (SBA) assist small business?

5. Describe the basic plan for starting a new business.

6. Discuss the advantages and disadvantages of a small business.

7. Are franchises a good investment? Why?

8. How has the shortage of venture capital caused people to turn to franchising?

9. How does the franchisor usually help a franchisee?

10. How does the franchisor maintain control of the franchisee?

11. Why have franchises grown in The United States?

12. Why have changes in American customs, working conditions and style of living led to a growth of fast food franchises?

*"Perfection of means and
confusion of ends seem
to characterize our age."*

-- Albert Einstein

SALES MANAGEMENT

A. Most principles of management are applicable to the area of sales management but due to the vast amount of selling in today's society, sales management should be looked at separately.

B. In most instances the area of personal selling is but a part of the firm's overall marketing objectives.
    1. Selling objectives differ from company to company depending in great part on the company's product and/or service and the customers they have and the potential customers they might attract.

C. The Sales Manager:
    1. Each sales manager has various objectives depending if he or she is the national sales manager, regional sales manager, and district sales manager. However, all objectives center about selling as much of the company's product and/or service as possible.
    2. The nature of the sales management job deals with a great deal of human interaction. The sales manager
        a. should be outgoing
        b. should be able to deal with people
        c. should be a problem solver
        d. should be able to motivate the sales force
        e. should be able to train salespeople
        f. should be a decisive decision maker
        g. should be results oriented
        h. should have knowledge of the salesperson's job
        i. should be energetic
        j. should be able to persuade
        k. should be organized.

D. The job of the salesperson:
    1. Searching out prospective customers.
    2. Finding out what the customer wants and needs.
    3. Fill the need of the customer.
    4. Gives sales presentations.
    5. Close the sale.
    6. Follow-up to satisfy customer and get new leads.

E. Compensation:
1. The sales manager should develop a system of compensation for the sales force. This is very important in getting productivity from the sales force.
2. Methods of compensation for sales force:
   a. salary
   b. commission
   c. salary + commission
   d. salary + bonus
   e. commission + bonus.

F. Methods of estimating sales:
1. Each salesperson estimates his or her future sales and these estimates are then added up.
2. Statistical analysis of company sales correlated with other economic indicators.
3. Study of sales during the previous years in order to notice trends.
4. Sampling the market and projecting sales.
5. Projecting the company's share of the industry wide market.
6. Educated guesses by executives and salespeople.

QUESTIONS FOR REVIEW AND DISCUSSION

1. Describe the main qualities that a sales manager should have?

2. Describe the job of the salesperson.

3. Which type of compensation is best for the sales force? Why?

*"Common sense in an
uncommon degree is what
the world calls wisdom."*

-- Samuel Taylor Coleridge

INTERNATIONAL MANAGEMENT

A. Firms, especially American firms look to get into the international trade area because they feel that there is a profit to be made in foreign trade.
    1. In dealing with other countries, there is no one true way to deal with them. Different countries have different methods of doing business and U. S. firms have to adopt to their methods.

B. Should a firm go into the international market?
    1. Before going into the international arena a firm must decide what its basic mission is.
        a. Is there a need for their goods?
        b. Can they buy goods cheaper in other countries?
        c. If they manufacture in a foreign country, does it pay for them?
        d. Is the foreign country's political situation stable enough to carry on business?

C. Key Terms of International Business:
    1. International Business - is any activity of a business that crosses international boundaries.
    2. Multinational corporation - one who operates a business in more than one country. e.g. the large oil companies.
        a. U. S. multinational corporations are very influential in the international business arena.
        b. In general, multinational corporations are becoming more and more international in the upper levels of management.
    3. Joint Venture - is a type of partnership consisting of (in an international operation) some nationals and some foreigners. In many cases it is the U. S. company that puts up the capital and citizens of the host country run the business. Of course, the American company has people there to help operate the business.
    4. Branch Office - is an extension of the firm's structure. It is an office away from the main headquarters of the firm. A branch office of the firm in the international arena is an office in a foreign country.

5. Subsidiary - is a firm which is owned (over 50%) by another firm. In the arena of international business, the subsidiary is organized under the laws of the nation in which it is conducting its business.
6. International Manager - a manager who is involved in international business activities.
7. Licensing - is the granting by a foreign nation to the firm to produce or distribute its products in that country.
8. Exporting - the selling of a firm's products to other countries.
9. Importing - the purchasing of products from other countries.
10. Balance of Trade - the relation of a nation's exports to imports. If you export more than you import you have a favorable balance of trade and vice-versa.
11. Balance of Payments - all transactions involving imports and exports, investments in plants and equipment, loans made by governments, foreign aid to nations, military spending and money deposits in foreign banks. It measures the amount of money coming into a country against the money going out of the country.
12. Protective Tariffs - a tax on imported goods with the purpose of protecting a nation's products by discouraging imports.
13. Revenue Tariff - a tax on imported goods in order to raise money (revenue).
14. Embargo - is a boycott that does not allow the importing of particular products.
15. Theory of Comparative Advantage - is a theory stating that each nation should concentrate on producing those goods it can supply most efficiently and inexpensively compared with other nations.
16. Specialization - the practice of a nation producing and trading the goods that it can supply most inexpensively and efficiently.
17. Capital-Intensive Economy - an economic system that uses methods of production that depends on large amounts of capital equipment.
18. Labor-Intensive Economy - an economic system that uses methods of production that depends on a large supply of cheap labor.
19. Tariff - a tax on imports entering the country.

20. International Cartel – a group of sellers of a pro-
      duct who join together to control the product's
      price, production and sale in order to obtain
      the advantages of a monopoly.

D. Three main obstacles that limit the amount of international
   trade.
   1. National Boundaries – distance from other coun-
         tries.
   2. Tariff Barriers – when a nation puts a tax
         (tariff) on imported goods to either raise
         money or protect its own industry or both.
   3. Nationalistic Barriers – appeal to national pride,
         loyalty to the workers of the country,
         quotas on imports and embargoes.

E. Free Trade versus Protectionism:
   1. Free Trade advocates believe that those nations
         that can produce particular items best should
         produce them at the cheapest price and should
         be allowed to sell these items on the open market.
   2. Protectionists believe that the country should pro-
         tect its industry and products. They want
         federal laws which serve to protect domestic
         industries from cheaper imported goods. Some
         examples of this are the U. S. textile industry
         and the U. S. auto industry.

F. Changes in international business over the years:
   1. During the era of European colonization of the
         western hemisphere, international business was
         based on the policy of mercantilism (the colo-
         nies of the conquering nation exist for the
         benefit of that nation and a nation's wealth is
         measured by the amount of gold and silver it
         possesses).
   2. The nature of international business was to exploit
         the colonies for the benefit of the mother
         country.
         a. Colonies as a source for raw materials.
         b. Colonies as a source of cheap labor.
         c. Colonies as a market for the nation's
               finished products.
   3. Individuals who served in the colonies carried the
         nation's culture to the outposts. This was
         very evident in the case of England and France
         in their colonies in Asia, North and South
         America and Africa.

179

4. The nationals serving in the colonies, along with the military saw as their purpose the protection of their nation's interests. However, the natives in the colonies began resenting the domination by the powerful nation and wanted an end to being exploited.

    a. Therefore, a gradual accommodation was made. Some mutual cooperation between the powerful nation and the colony was developed.

    b. Because (even after gaining independence) the colony or former colony needed the powerful countries money, technological know-how and economic understanding; some sort of compromise was agreed to with each country becoming a partner in the various business enterprises.

    c. Eventually, the strong companies of the powerful country were replaced by multi-national corporations in which the powerful country's executives are used in top management positions while the local people are used in lower positions.

G. Advantages and Disadvantages of International Business:

Advantages	Disadvantages
(1) High rate of profit.	(1) Low rate of profit.
(2) Stability.	(2) Forced into a joint venture that is high risk.
(3) Learning a foreign culture.	(3) Methods of doing business in the other country that is harmful to the firm.
(4) Cooperation with foreign governments.	
(5) New areas of developments.	(4) Possibility of nationalizing the business.
	(5) Need to adopt to foreign culture.
	(6) Red-tape.
	(7) Interference of foreign government.

H. Type of people assigned to international positions:
1. Should be experienced.
2. Should be mature.
3. Should be tolerant.
4. Should be willing to learn about other cultures.
5. Should enjoy traveling.
6. Should have a great degree of competency in their particular field.
7. Should be optimistic.
8. Should be able to have others trust him or her.

I. Conflicts of cultures affects international managers.
1. When managers deal in a different culture, they face different methods of doing things and different expectations. They must adapt to these differences and make the necessary adjustments in order to successfully conduct the business of the firm.
2. Cultural Differences
   a. Ethnocentrism - is the using of one's own culture as the criteria of reference in dealing with a foreign culture.
      1) If this is done by international managers it will most likely be resented by the native population and harm business.
      2) A different value system has to be adjusted to the foreign value system. If this can be done, the firm stands a chance for greater success. If it can't, then the chance for success is greatly diminished.
   b. Religious differences - different religious customs can have a great effect on the firm's business.
   c. Differences in customs and various society's norms of behavior contribute to cultural differences.
   d. The international manager's inability to adjust to, or unwillingness to adjust to cultural differences often cause difficulties.
      1) harms relations with local personnel of firm.

2) harms relations with local
customers of firm.
3) harms relations with local
government of host
country.

J.   Economic Differences:
1. <u>Technological differences</u> - different nations are in
different situations in regard to the degree of
development in the technological area.
2. <u>Economic philosophy</u> - differences in economic philosophy can influence the host nation's treatment of the firm.
3. <u>Demographic influences</u> - differences in the influence of population can also influence the host
nation's treatment of the company.
4. <u>Standard of living of the native population</u> - if a
host nation has a much lower standard of living
it can lead to a great deal of resentment towards the firm of the investor nation.
5. <u>Modes of labor of the native work force</u> - if the
host nation has people who are only able to do
menial labor and cannot handle some of the
modern equipment, the investor company has to
invest a great deal of time, effort and money in
order to train a productive labor force.
6. <u>Rate of productivity of work force</u> - if the host
nation has a work force that is highly productive, it will encourage foreign investment to
build industry there and vice-versa.
7. <u>Rate of currency exchange</u> - if the investor nation
gets a good rate of exchange in the host country, it will be a source of encouragement to do
business in that country.

K. Political Differences:
1. The nature of the international political scene can
have a great effect on the success of a firm.
For example, when Fidel Castro came to power
in Cuba, he nationalized a number of businesses owned by U. S. firms.
2. <u>Foreign policy</u> - the foreign policy of the U. S.
can effect the firm. For instance, the government might not want a firm to do business in a
particular country or may not want them to
send certain types of products to that country.
The U. S. government does not want U. S.
firms to export high technological items to The
Soviet Union.

3. <u>National prejudices</u> – this can vary as the international scene will vary.

QUESTIONS FOR REVIEW AND DISCUSSION

1. Why does a firm go into international business?

2. Explain:
   a) joint venture
   b) multinational corporation
   c) balance of trade
   d) economic boycott
   e) balance of payments
   f) free trade
   g) protectionism

3. How can international business benefit a firm?

4. Which type of people are best suited to positions in international business?

5. How do cultural differences influence the international manager's actions?

6. How do economic differences influence the actions of the international manager?

7. How do political differences affect the actions of the international manager?

"It ain't over till it's over."

-- *Yogi Berra*

MANAGEMENT FOR CHANGE

A. Managers will manage change:
    1. The one constant in management is that there will be change. In addition as the rate of technology increases and the rate of knowledge increases the rate of change will also increase. The manager will have to learn to adopt to change and help his subordinates make changes and adjust to the various changes that will be made.
    2. Change is a major part of any organization.
        a. Change is any alteration that occurs within the organization.

B. People are resistant to change:
    1. The introduction of change in any firm is not easy. Workers develop set ways of doing things and prefer to remain doing the familiar operations rather than the unfamiliar. People are resistant to change for some of the following reasons:
        a. Fear of failure.
        b. Fear that change will make it more difficult for them to function.
        c. Change can be inconvenient.
        d. Lack of clarity in making the change.
        e. Uncertainty.
        f. The rate of change can be too rapid.
        g. Change can bring about threats to social relationships that have developed on the job.
        h. Information is not related in a clear manner to subordinates.
        i. There is not enough subordinate participation in making the changes.

C. Ways of reducing resistance to change:
    1. Increase participation.
    2. Reassurance that the subordinates interests will not be overlooked.
    3. One should not initiate change for change's sake. Change should be meaningful. If change is shown to be meaningful than there will be greater cooperation in the change.
    4. Prepare the subordinates for change.

5. It is important that the subordinates trust the judgement of the manager. If they do, co-operation in the change will be much easier.
6. Good communication is very important. Certain types of questions must be explained to the subordinates.
    a. What type of change is being made?
    b. Why is the change being made?
    c. Which employees will be affected by the change?
    d. When will the change take place?
    e. How will the change be put into operation?
    f. Who will be responsible for the change?
7. Explain the change fully to all those being affected.

D. The Steps of Change:
    1. Edgar H. Schein, a psychologist, sets up the following model in an article called "Management as a Process of Influence," Industrial Management (May, 1961), 59-70.
        a. Unfreezing - this occurs when people are willing to learn.
        b. Changing - this occurs when people are willing to change.
        c. Refreezing - is the final acceptance so that the new changes become a permanent integrative part of the person.
    2. Kurt Lewin's model of change has three basic steps:
        a. Unfreeze - move away from old modes of behavior.
        b. Move - the person moves to a new type of position.
        c. Refreeze - the new behavior is then re-frozen.

E. Change is a difficult concept to many people. Good managers have to be able to lead change when necessary and inspire and obtain the trust of subordinates to follow the manager in bringing about change.

QUESTIONS FOR REVIEW AND DISCUSSION

1. Why do people resist change?

2. How can a manager reduce resistance to change?

3. When should change be brought about?

4. "Change should not be made for change's sake." Explain.

SELECTED BIBLIOGRAPHY

BOOKS

Antony, Jay. Management and Machiavelli. New York: Holt, Rinehart and Winston, 1967.

Argyris, Chris. Personality and Organization: The Conflict Between the System and the Individual. New York: Harper & Row, 1957.

Barnard, C. I. The Functions of the Executive. Cambridge, Mass.: Harvard University Press, 1938.

Bedeian, Arthur G. and Glueck, William F. Management. Hinsdale, Ill.: Dryden Press, 1983.

Blake, Robert R. and Mouton, Jane S. The Managerial Grid. Houston: Gulf Publishing Co.: 1964.

Boone, Louis E. and Kurtz, David L. Principles of Management, 2nd Edition. New York: Random House, 1984.

Carroll, Jr., Stephen J. and Tosi, Jr., Henry L. Management by Objectives: Applications and Research. New York: Macmillan & Co., 1973.

Cleland, David I. and King, William R. Systems Analysis and Project Management. New York: McGraw-Hill Book Co., 1968.

Dale, Ernest. Management: Theory and Practice. New York: McGraw-Hill Book Co., 1965.

Davis, R. C. The Fundamentals of Top Management. New York: Harper & Brothers, 1951.

Drucker, Peter F. The Practice of Management. New York: Harper & Row, 1954.

Drucker, Peter F. Concept of the Corporation. New York: The John Day Company, 1972.

Fayol, Henri. General and Industrial Management. London: Pitman Publishing Corp., 1949.

Fiedler, Fred E. A Theory of Leadership Effectiveness. New York: McGraw-Hill Book Co., 1967.

Friedman, Milton. Capitalism and Freedom. Chicago: University of Chicago Press, 1962.

Gantt, Henry L. Organizing for Work. London: George Allen and Unwin, 1919.

Geneen, Harold. Managing. New York: Doubleday & Co., 1984.

Gulick, L. and Urwick L. (eds.). Papers on the Science of Administration. New York: Institute of Public Administration, 1937.

Hampton, John J. Financial Decision-Making. Reston, VA.: Reston Publishing Co., 1976.

Herzberg, Frederick, Mausner, B. and Snyderman, B. The Motivation to Work. New York: John Wiley and Sons, 1959.

Kohn, Mervin. Dynamic Managing. Menlo Park, California: Cummings Publishing Co., Inc., 1977.

Koontz, Harold and O'Donnell, Cyril. Principles of Management. New York: McGraw-Hill Book Co., 1955.

Koontz, Harold and O'Donnell, Cyril. Essentials of Management. New York: McGraw-Hill Book Co., 1974.

Leavitt, Harold. Managerial Psychology. 2nd Edition. Chicago: University of Chicago Press, 1964.

Levinson, Harry. The Great Jackass Fallacy. Boston: Division of Research, Graduate School of Business Administrtion, Harvard University, 1973.

Likert, Rensis. New Patterns of Management. New York: McGraw-Hill Book Co., 1961.

Litwin, George H. and Stringer, Jr., Robert A. Motivation and Organizational Climate. Boston: Division of Research, Graduate School of Business Administration, Harvard University, 1968.

Longenecker, Justin G. Essentials of Management. Columbus, Ohio: Charles E. Merrill Publishing Co., 1977.

Maier, Norman R. *Psychology in Industrial Organizations*. Boston, Mass.: Houghton-Mifflin & Co., 1973.

Maslow, Abraham H. *Motivation and Personality*. New York: Harper and Brothers, 1954.

Mayo, Elton. *The Human Problems of an Industrial Civilization*. Boston: Division of Research, Harvard Business School, 1945.

McClelland, David C. *The Achieving Society*. Princeton, N. J.: Van Nostrand, 1961.

McGregor, Douglas. *The Human Side of Enterprise*. New York: McGraw-Hill Book Co., 1960.

McGregor, Douglas. *The Professional Manager*. New York: McGraw-Hill Book Co., 1967.

Murphy, Edward F. *Management vs. The Unions*. New York: Stein and Day, 1971.

Newman, William H. and Warren, E. Kirby. *The Process of Management*. 4th Edition. Englewood Cliffs, N. J.: Prentice-Hall, 1977.

Ouchi, William G. *Theory Z*. Reading, Mass.: Addison-Wesley, 1981.

Parkinson, C. N. *Parkinson's Law*. Boston: Houghton-Mifflin, 1957.

Peter, Lawrence F. and Hull, Raymond. *The Peter Principle*. New York: William Morrow, 1969.

Sherman, Jr., A. W. *Personnel Management*. 5th Edition. Cincinnati: Southwestern Publishing Co., 1976.

Skinner, B. F. *Science and Human Behavior*. New York: The Free Press, 1953.

Stanton, William J. and Buskirk, Richard H. *Management of the Sales Force*. Homewood, Ill.: Richard D. Irwin, Inc., 1974.

Taylor, Frederick W. *The Principles of Scientific Management*. New York: Harper and Brothers, 1911.

193

Terry, George R. Principles of Management. Homewood, Illinois: Richard D. Irwin, 1977.

U. S. Government Printing Office. Statistical Abstract of the United States. Published yearly.

von Bertalanffy, Ludwig. General Systems Theory. New York: George Braziller, 1969.

Vroom, Victor H. Work and Motivation. New York: J. Wiley and Sons, Inc., 1964.

Vroom, Victor H. and Yetton, Philip W. Leadership and Decicion-Making. Pittsburgh: University of Pittsburgh Press, 1973.

Woodward, Joan. Industrial Organization: Theory and Practice. London: Oxford University Press, 1965.

Wren, Daniel A. The Evolution of Management Thought. New York: Ronald Press, 1972.

ARTICLES

Blake, Robert R., Mouton, Jane S., Barnes, Louis B. and Grenier, Larry E. "Breakthrough in Organization Development." Harvard Business Review (Nov.-Dec., 1964), 133-155.

Greenwood, Ronald C. "Management by Objectives: As Developed by Peter Drucker, assisted by Harold Smiddy." Academy of Management Review (April, 1981), 225-230.

Grenier, Larry E. "Patterns of Organization Change." Harvard Business Review (May-June, 1967), 119-130.

Henry, Porter. "Manage Your Sales Force as a System." Harvard Business Review (March-April, 1975), 85-95.

Koontz, Harold. "The Management Theory Jungle." Journal of the Academy of Management (Vol. 4, No. 3) 174-188.

Kotkin, Joel and Kishimoto, Yoriko. "Theory F", Inc., (April, 1986), 52-60.

Levinson, Harry. "Management by Whose Objectives?" Harvard Business Review (July-August, 1970), 125-134.

Maslow, Abraham H. "A Theory of Human Motivation." Psychological Review (July, 1943), 370-396.

McKenney, James L. and Keen, Peter G. W. "How Manager's Minds Work." Harvard Business Review (April, 1981), 225-230.

Schein, Edgar H. "Management as a Process of Influence," Industrial Management Review (May, 1961), 59-76.

Tannenbaum, Robert and Schmidt, Warren H. "How to Choose a Leadership Pattern." Harvard Business Review (March-April, 1958), 95-101.

PERIODICALS

The Wall Street Journal

Dun's Business Monthly

Forbes

Barron's

Boardroom Reports

Business Week

Inc.

Fortune

Journal of Accountancy

Harvard Business Review

Journal of Business

Journal of Marketing

Nation's Business

Survey of Current Business

INDEX